IAN R MITCHELL is an historian, who gave up teaching to devote himself to writing full time. After graduating from university in his native Aberdeen, Ian did postgraduate research at Leeds, followed by a British Council scholarship to study in Berlin. The author of articles in learned journals, and of a standard textbook on Bismarck, taught for over twenty years at Clydebank College history. Increasingly interested in Sco a lifelong hillwalker, Ian has produced s Scotland's Mountains before the Mountai explorations and ascents in the Scottish mountai writes frequently on outdoor matters for climbing journals and the general media. In addition, he gives talks and slide shows on his books. Ian has lived in Glasgow since 1973.

This City Now

Glasgow and its working class past

IAN R MITCHELL

Luath Press Limited
EDINBURGH
www.luath.co.uk

First published 2005

Extracts from Edwin Morgan's poem *King Billy* from his *New Selected Poems* (2000) and from Hugh MacDiarmid's poems *Second Hymn to Lenin*, *Third Hymn to Lenin* and *A Drunk Man Looks at the Thistle* from his *Complete Poems* (1993) reproduced by permission of Carcanet Press Limited.

Extracts from Dorothy Paul's *Revelations of a Rejected Soprano* and John Cairney's *East End to West End: First Steps in an Autobiographical Journey* reproduced by kind permission of Mainstream Publishing.

Extracts from Ralph Glasser's *Growing up in the Gorbals* reproduced by kind permission of Pan MacMillan.

The paper used in this book is recyclable. It is made from low chlorine pulps produced in a low energy, low emission manner from renewable forests.

Maps by Jim Lewis

Printed and bound by
Bell & Bain Ltd., Glasgow

Typeset in Sabon 12 by Sarah Crozier, Nantes

To Mungo's Bairns

Spirit of Lenin, light on this city now!

Light up this city now!

Hugh MacDiarmid, 'Third Hymn to Lenin'

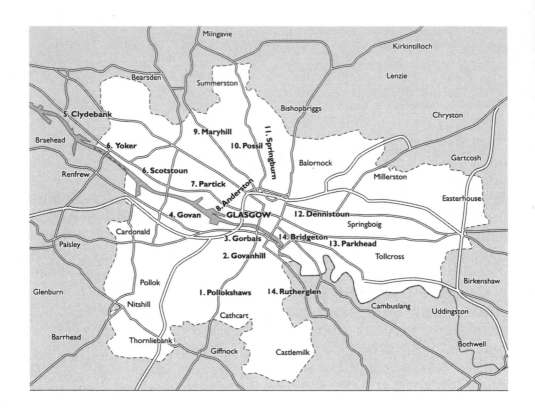

Milngavie

Kirkintilloch

Bearsden

Summerston

Lenzie

Bishopbriggs

5. Clydebank

Chryston

Braehead

9. Maryhill

11. Springburn

10. Possil

Gartcosh

6. Yoker

Balornock

Renfrew

6. Scotstoun

Millerston

Easterhouse

7. Partick

8. Anderston

4. Govan

GLASGOW

12. Dennistoun

Springboig

Cardonald

3. Gorbals

14. Bridgeton

13. Parkhead

Paisley

2. Govanhill

Tollcross

Birkenshaw

Pollok

1. Pollokshaws

14. Rutherglen

Glenburn

Nitshill

Cathcart

Cambuslang

Uddingston

Barrhead

Thornliebank

Giffnock

Castlemilk

Bothwell

Contents

Foreword

THIS CITY NOW sets out to retrieve the hidden architectural, cultural and historical riches of some of Glasgow's working-class districts. Many who enjoy the fruits of Glasgow's recent gentrification will be surprised and delighted by the gems which Ian R Mitchell has uncovered beyond the usual haunts. The denizens of Glasgow's West End, its suburbs, and even some of the inhabitants of the districts which he has reclaimed will look with fresh eyes on areas previously designated as 'urban deserts' or 'wastelands'. For example, how many of us knew that Govan Old Parish Church is home to one of the oldest and most important collections of early Christian sculpture in Scotland, or that in Springburn can be found a semi-detached villa designed by Charles Rennie Mackintosh?

However, this book is not only an attempt to reinsert into public consciousness the architectural and cultural delights of Glasgow's working-class areas. It also recaptures the social and political history of the working classes of those districts; so that the narrative is braided with tales of Calton's weavers, Govan and Partick's wartime rent-strikes, and the colliers and weavers of Parkhead, who, it seems, were early pioneers of the right-to-roam movement.

Ian R Mitchell's affection for his adopted city shines through every page of this book. He has lived in Glasgow exactly the same number of years as I have, yet his knowledge and appreciation of the city put me to shame. More importantly, the book has inspired me to put on my walking boots and head for Govan Road, Bridgeton Cross and Tollcross Park. I am sure it will have the same effect on many of its readers.

Eleanor Gordon
Professor of Gender and Social History
University of Glasgow

Glasgow Despite Them

AS MOUNTAINS CAN BE seen as the supreme work of nature, so is the city the greatest work of human geology, the high point of social and cultural evolution. For the Greeks and Romans the *polis* was the social ideal and the citizen its representative. For the early and later Christians Heaven was a city, and in the Renaissance the city-state embodied the humanistic strivings of the era. For the Victorians too, despite the development of rural romanticism, civic pride was a central driving force in their achievements.

A great city (the Germans use the term *Weltstadt*) is qualitatively different from a small one; a critical mass is needed to transform the parochial into the cosmopolitan – though other things are needed too. Not every big city is a *Weltstadt*, indeed most are not. A *Weltstadt* is one which has had a clear impact on world history, and where the main issues of its epoch, intellectual, social and political, have been posed. James Watt's invention of the steam engine and the launching of the industrialisation and urbanisation of the western world alone would make Glasgow a *Weltstadt*. But we should not forget that, though now small on the city scale, at the beginning of the twentieth century when it produced two British prime ministers, Glasgow was in the top ten metropolises in Europe. Over one million people then lived in the Second City of the Empire. And the key political questions of the early twentieth century (imperialism, war, revolution) were more clearly posed in Glasgow than anywhere else in Britain. The former Second City may now only be fourth in the United Kingdom after Birmingham and Manchester; but they were never world cities. Edinburgh, however, was – though back in the eighteenth century.

I appreciated Glasgow – though not uncritically – before it was Miles Better. I moved here over 30 years ago when it appeared as if the city were dying. De-industrialisation had begun, as had depopulation. The city had a very negative image and even amongst its own population low civic esteem was prevalent. The buildings were still being indiscriminately flattened, and I recall that there were only a handful of them stone-cleaned and restored. The architecture (mainly in its Victorian expressions) fascinated me. The city's skyline against the ever-varying cloud patterns of its dominant southwesterlies created drama which constantly drew me onto the city street. I grew to appreciate the blue-black sky against the multistorey blocks of the Red Road, dawn emerging behind the Necropolis in winter, and Park Circus glowing on a summer's evening, as much as I did a Cuillin sunset, or morning on the winter plateau of the Cairngorms.

The culture of Glasgow also attracted me, and not just in the sense of the availability of theatre and art, things belatedly recognised when Glasgow became European City of Culture in 1990 and City of Architecture in 1999. Glasgow is probably the only place in Britain where, even imperfectly, there is a working-class cultural dominance, which constantly refers back to itself and its own history rather than to the rural hinterland of its origins, as the working-class culture of Aberdeen, for example, tends to do. This is not to exaggerate and elevate the consciousness of the Glasgow workers to something greater than it is or was, but still this is a city dominated by its working class and the history of their organisations and struggles. Often this is forgotten and sterrheid schmaltz is passed off as Glasgow working-class culture.

'The glory of Glasgow is in what the unknown working class districts contain,' said James Hamilton Muir in *Glasgow in 1901*, written to mark the Empire Exhibition of that year when the city was at its apogee. Although that book did not quite live up to its promise of revealing these glories, I take its comment as my starting point. *This City Now* looks at the development of some of the main working-class areas of Glasgow from their origins till the time when it was a world city, and follows their subsequent evolution. Most of these areas were independent communities, swallowed up by Glasgow's growth and to some extent left behind by its decline, and to the familiar pattern of inner-city decay. Most too still retain their local identities. I have chosen areas which have a story to tell, in relation to the history of the Glasgow working class, its industries, struggles, organisations and noteable personalities. In addition I am convinced that the social significance of areas like Govan, Bridgeton and Springburn, along with the other inner-city districts treated in this work, is in many cases matched by their little-known historical and architectural heritage.

The experience of urban rambling is sadly underrated, and mainly limited to the obviously tourist cities. This was not always the case, and before 1950 exploration in our industrial cities was more widespread. In Glasgow, for example, there are many books from half a century ago and more, giving its inhabitants tips about, and guides to, places to walk. James Cowan's *From Glasgow's Treasure Chest* (1933) is an example of a genre which goes back at least to John Tweed's *Guide to Glasgow and the Clyde* of 1872. However the rise of the motor car – and possibly the decline of civic pride in our industrial cities which have undergone painful transformation in the last half century as industry and population moved out – seems to have all but killed off this tradition of urban walking – and writing about urban walking. With the Urban Renaissance going on around us in our increasingly post-industrial cities, including Glasgow, there are signs of a welcome re-invention of this tradition.

Glasgow, as are many big cities, is like a series of medium sized towns, whose inhabitants overlap at the city centre, or at places such as football grounds. This was even more so in the days when industries were identified with areas, and inhabitants of specific areas tended to work locally. This multiplicity of apparent parochialisms, is overlain, however, with a very strong sense of city identity. Whether from Parkhead or Partick, the ruling motto is 'Glasgow belongs to me' – and there are no no-go areas for the Glasgow working class. In Edinburgh, on the other hand, the city centre belongs to the middle classes and to the tourists, the working class remaining ghettoed in its Bantustans. I recall being in Rogano's, one of Glasgow's top restaurants, when a punter entered, and, on discovering he could not purchase a pint of Tennent's lager, left, but with the dismissive comment to the waiter that 'Ye could dae wi a band in here, son, tae liven things up.' The restaurant was at fault, not him.

Dr Johnson, when he visited Scotland in the mid-eighteenth century, said that most Scots knew as little of the Highlands as they did of Borneo. The same might be said today about Glasgow, not only of

Glasgow's increasing tourist traffic, but of many of its own inhabitants – especially its suburban ones. They may well be familiar with
the West End, or the city centre and Merchant City, but with little
else. The city limits are the new Borneo, ignored, or driven through at
speed. Johnson also said of the Highlanders, 'All they have left is their
language and their poverty,' and many might be tempted to repeat
this of Govan or Bridgeton today. But it was not true for the
Highlanders two hundred years ago, though Johnson's intellectual
limitations prevented him seeing this. And neither is it true for the
inhabitants of Glasgow's Victorian and Edwardian industrial areas
today. TC Smout, a historian I admire, could print a photograph of
Ibrox Stadium in 1921 in his *Century of the Scottish People*, and cap-
tion it 'Ibrox in its Urban Desert'. One would have to enquire what
Smout knew of Govan when he wrote this. He was clearly ignorant of
Govan's Gaelic Choir, its 250-year-old Govan Fair, or its unique collection of incised medieval sculpture in Govan Old Kirk. Govan, or
Bridgeton, or Springburn – all these working-class areas had choirs,
clubs, bands, societies and a richer cultural life, one would say
without hesitation, than many a suburban development.

Finding this world can be adventurous. While much can be assimi-
lated from reading, it is by wandering around on foot you get the feel
of any place. Walter Benjamin wrote of his urban rambles in interwar Paris that he was 'botanising the asphalt'. I see my urban walking
as 'politicising the pavements'. There is an undeniable edge to walking in Glasgow because of the proximity of different social classes in
certain borderlands. There are places where you can turn left or right
from pub, shop, café – even a tenement close – and be in different
worlds. In one direction you can be somewhere where apartments
cost £300,000 and in another direction, within a few steps, nothing
seems to cost more than £1. Redevelopment has created areas where
the two worlds are intermingled, without apparently fusing, for
example in Calton. It is in areas like this that you realise the accuracy
of what Baudelaire, a dedicated urban walker, said: 'What are the
dangers of the forest and the prairie compared with the daily shocks
and conflicts of civilisation?' In an age of increasing painting-by-
numbers travel, the urban edge has a claim to being one of the
remaining frontiers.

4

In most areas though, urban geography separates, rather than mingles, social classes. Walking about you see how urban planners and consumer 'choice' have largely segregated working-class from middle-class areas by a series of rivers, canals, railways (hence the phrase 'wrong side of the tracks') and larger roads, almost as complete as any apartheid. Parks also tend to enforce social segregation, establishing an acceptable physical distance between high and low-income social groups. Working-class areas, however, tend to flow more into one another, do not tend to be so brutally divided from each other as they are from the middle-class areas, but pounding the asphalt you soon realise that districts that appear to coalesce are sharply defined, in a way that driving or going by bus does not reveal.

The identity of specific areas is created in many ways. Of course there is the labelling established by libraries, post offices, street names, names of parks and schools, which tells you that you are in Govan or Gorbals. Wall murals and gang slogans are another way of defining territory. People meeting in cafés, pubs and shops define a geosocial nexus, as did, in the past, local workplaces. The physical and the mental combine to produce definite *quartiers*. People know where they are. Everone will tell you that the Duke Street railway divides Dennistoun from Bridgeton. I stood on one side of the road photographing the high flats of Pollokshaws on the other, and was informed by someone, who surely knew, that where I was standing wasn't the Shaws – though I was only across the road from what I photographed. At meetings I attended over the restoration of Maryhill Burgh Halls, the locals discoursed intensely over not only what was Maryhill, but of the boundaries of its subdivisions, Gairbraid, Wyndford and Cadder.

I have been discovering this city for 30 years. Some districts are still relatively little known to me, including some of the older working-class settlements such as Shettleston, which is a little far from where I live to walk to casually. There are postwar housing estates like Castlemilk where I have never set foot – though I do know Drumchapel quite well. William Faulkner, the Mississipi novelist, said he would never exhaust his postage stamp of southern soil; I feel it would take several lifetimes to exhaust Glasgow, which still surprises, amazes, delights and angers in turn. These are all emotions I would wish to hold on to and which are stimulated by residence here.

In 1951 Glasgow, or 'The Dear Green Place', according to a possible translation of its original Gaelic name, still had over a million people. Since the 1960s Glasgow has haemorrhaged population; today there are about 625,000 inhabitants. Over a period of three decades Glasgow has lost population at a rate of almost 10,000 a year. Put another way, that means that in each decade since 1970 Glasgow lost more population that the entire Highlands during the whole century of Highland Clearances. There are signs, however, that this fall is bottoming out: 2003 was the first year for over three decades in which the city's population did not decline. We get volumes of poetry about the Highland Clearances; but where are the sonnets to the silent stones of Springburn? True, the population of Springburn or Govan or Bridgeton was not forced onto boats and didn't have their roofs burned over their heads, but there was no alternative to leaving. If all had stayed, today Glasgow's unemployment rate would be on the levels of Calcutta or Cairo. Much of the skilled working class was forced to leave the city to find work in other parts of Scotland or abroad, but much of the upper and middle classes left by choice. Unwilling to pay Glasgow's rates and later council tax, and unwilling to have their children mix with Mungo's bairns, these people moved out to the suburbs, through still parasiting on the city. Half of Glasgow's working population live outwith the city boundaries, many actually employed by the city council, and these middle classes are disproportionate users of the city's cultural and other facilities. Today Glasgow is a city of lower professionals such as teachers and social workers and other intellectual and cultural workers, and of unskilled workers and the increasingly hereditary underclass. Its industrial base has declined to about 30,000 employees and its industrial glory has gone forever. It is a Naples of the North.

Despite being abandoned by its own bourgeoisie and middle class (with the exception of its intellectual sector which embraces working-class cultural and political values to a great extent), and despite the machinations of the Edinburgh establishment in issues like boundary revisions, Glasgow has come through a period of economic decline alive and moderately kicking. Glasgow may not have flourished, but Glasgow has survived – despite them, and at least in part because of the resilience bred of its working-class culture. I said above that the silent stones of Springburn have not inspired any sonnets, but they and the others of this city have inspired this book. I hope it will light up this city now, and open many eyes to its fascination.

Pollokshaws

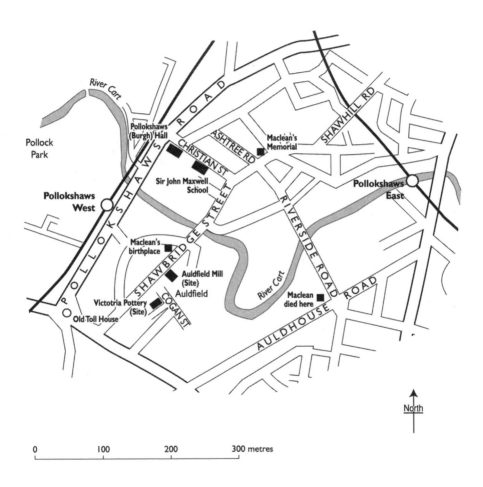

River Cart

Pollock Park

Pollokshaws West

Old Toll House

Victotria Pottery (Site)

Maclean's birthplace

Sir John Maxwell School

Pollokshaws (Burgh) Hall

POLLOKSHAWS ROAD

CHRISTIAN ST

ASHTREE RD

Maclean's Memorial

SHAWHILL RD

Pollokshaws East

GE STREET

SHAWBRIDGE

COGAN ST

Auldfield Mill (Site)

Auldfield

River Cart

RIVERSIDE ROAD

Maclean died here

AULDHOUSE ROAD

North

| 0 | 100 | 200 | 300 metres |

CHAPTER ONE

John Maclean's Pollokshaws

ON 1 DECEMBER 1923, 5,000 people marched four miles south from Eglinton Toll in Glasgow to Eastwood cemetery, passing through the district of Pollokshaws. Possibly the most loved – and probably also the most hated – man in Scotland, John Maclean, had died. Another 10,000 lined the streets to pay tribute to a person whose life ended prematurely at 44 from overwork, the effects of imprisonment and – eventually – from near-starvation. Fifty years thereafter, in 1973, a memorial was erected near the Old Town House of Pollokshaws, to the district's most famous son, which stated simply:

> In Memory of John Maclean
> Born in Pollokshaws on 24th August 1879
> Died 30th November 1923
> FAMOUS PIONEER OF WORKING CLASS EDUCATION
> HE FORGED THE SCOTTISH LINK IN THE
> GOLDEN LINK OF WORLD SOCIALISM.

When Maclean was born, Pollokshaws was a village, though an expanding one, still outwith Glasgow's city boundaries; in fact it was in the Eastwood district of Renfrewshire. Though its origins go back to medieval times, it began to assume importance in the later eighteenth century as a textile-weaving town, using the water power of the River Cart and its subsidiary, the Auldhouse Burn. By the mid-nineteenth century several weaving factories had been established in the village as well as print and dye works, the Auldhouse and Cart often running red with the dyes poured into them. It was never a classic tenement area, but a mix of pre and post-industrial and semirural buildings, many of which were in worse condition than the tenements of areas like Govan and Bridgeton.

The main landed family in this area were the Maxwells of Pollok, whose mansion house lay in what is now Pollok Park to the west of 'the Shaws'. Though landed proprietors, the Maxwells, like many others, eventually became more dependent on their industrial than their agricultural wealth, and they opened or leased many coal mines on their lands, and took an active part in developing the textile industries of Pollokshaws itself. When Maclean was born the Maxwells still wielded enormous power in the burgh as employers, kirk patrons and as office-bearers on the burgh council and its various agencies. This only really began to decline when the Shaws was annexed to Glasgow in 1912. The Maxwell family on their adjoining estate lived on almost exactly the same amount of land as was occupied by the 12,000 people of the Shaws; such was the wealth gap in Victorian Britain. Incidentally Maclean approved of the annexation of the Shaws by Glasgow. Indeed one of his constant political demands was the extension of the city boundaries to include its contiguous urban areas; a demand as relevant today as it was 100 years ago.

Maclean was born at 59 King Street, just south of the Shawbrig over the Cart, and a street now subsumed by Shawbridge Road. His parents were both immigrants to Pollokshaws, and both victims of the process of clearance and famine which drove many Highlanders to come to Glasgow in the mid-nineteenth century. His father, Daniel, was a potter who came to Glasgow from Mull, after a spell working at Bo'ness. He worked in the Victoria Pottery of Lockhart and Sons in Cogan Street, a couple of minutes walk from King Street: the works opened in 1855 and finally closed in 1952. Daniel died in 1888 from silicosis ('potter's lung'). The Victoria Pottery occupied the land now given over to the car park of the Auldhouse Retail Park.

Daniel's death left John's mother, Anne, to look after four children. Anne had married Daniel at the nearby mining village of Nitshill in 1867. As a child Anne had walked with her mother, neither speaking a word of English, from Corpach near Fort William to join her own father working as a quarryman in Paisley. She had been a weaver before marriage and resumed this trade as a widow at the Auldfield Mill, which lay just across the road in Cogan Street from where her husband Daniel had worked. The mill was opened by John Cogan in 1851, and occupied the present vacant lot next to the Comet store car park. The village character of the Shaws at this time was emphasised by the fact that the Macleans' Church, the Original Secession Church, lay just round the corner from Cogan Street, in Shawbridge Street. The building is presently the parish kirk of Pollokshaws. The Shaws was a small world in those days, with the part south of the Shawbrig where the Macleans lived, worked and prayed being almost a village within a village.

Religion played a far greater part in Victorian working-class life than it subsequently has, and in the Shaws there were ten churches, a Catholic one, and the others representing every variety of Protestant denomination: Established Kirk, Free Kirk, various Secession Churches and even a Methodist chapel. The 1895 street map of the burgh also shows a dozen public houses in the short stretch between the Old Town House and the Shawbrig, and the pub was the other pole of working-class life to the kirk in the years before 1900. Maclean was to become a fierce opponent both of religion and of alcohol (though he was never a campaigning teetotaller, seeing drunkenness as the result, not the cause, of working-class misery.) He looked to provide the working man with better fare for mind and body – working-class education in Marxist political and economic principles – and Maclean spent his free time not in the kirk or the pub but in Pollokshaws Public Library. Though his boyhood Calvinism lapsed, his associated belief in the overriding importance of education never waned. Calvinists believed a study of the Bible must lead to God; with equal fervour Maclean believed the study of Marx must lead to socialism. Maclean is often portrayed as a violent revolutionary. In fact he believed that Marxist education would eventually lead to a peaceful triumph for socialism at the ballot box, and that violence need only be used in self-defence.

Maclean's own education was interesting. He first attended Pollok Academy, which had been established as an elementary school through the efforts of the Burgh council and Sir John Maxwell, 8th Bart. This was built in 1856 and was part designed by Alexander 'Greek' Thomson. It lay on Pollokshaws Road, just opposite the present entrance to Pollok Park, on the presently vacant site south of the Burgh Hall. It was later converted to a secondary school, and eventually demolished in the 1960s. This school was again only a couple of minutes from the Macleans' King Street home – though for his secondary education John had to leave the Shaws and go to Queens Park Secondary. But this did not end his connection with the schools and schoolmasters of Pollokshaws.

Maclean undertook his teacher's training at the Free Kirk Seminary at Trinity in Glasgow's Park Circus area from 1898–1900; he walked from the Shaws to Trinity every day, a round distance of ten miles. Later he did his MA via evening classes at Glasgow University, again using shanks' pony, apparently in a deliberate attempt to maintain his fitness, as well as to save cash. His father's death and his brother's developing tuberculosis had a deep effect on him. He worked as a message boy for various shops in the Shaws and also as a caddie on the nearby Thornliebank Golf Course, which doubtless developed his pedestrian abilities, as did his postie round on student holidays. Maclean was a typical lapsed Calvinist in that he could not be idle, he always had to be doing something. On the few short holidays he took in his life, he usually fretted to return to his propaganda work in Glasgow.

Subsequent to his father's death, followed by the marriage of his sisters and his brother's emigration to South Africa, Maclean moved with his mother to Low Cartcraigs in the Shaws. This was a small cluster of pre-industrial housing and workshops, such as a smiddy which lay across Pollokshaws Road (between the road and the railway) from the Old Toll House. Anne had given up work in the mill, and took in a lodger as well as having John's earnings once he became a teacher.

Low Cartcraigs is now occupied by the western portion of the Pollokshaws Road dual carriageway, but the Old Toll House, dating from around 1800 still stands. It was occupied as a dwelling house till the late 1950s. It lost its original function with the abolition of road tolls and became a public house, serving the horse races which were held nearby till 1838. These races led to a poem from a mother warning her son against temptation:

Said she, 'Ye may be trod to death
Beneath the horses' paws
And mind ye, lad, the sayin's true
There's queer folk i' the Shaws.'

Many of the good folk of the Shaws around 1900 would probably have recalled that saying as their village was assailed by the preachings of a new set of queer folk – the socialists. Indeed Maclean's conversion to socialism took place largely within the intellectual structures of his native Shaws – and surprisingly active and varied these were too.

In 1900 Maclean joined the Progressive Union in Pollokshaws, an organisation which discussed issues such as socialism, anarchism, the natural sciences and social problems generally. Its main aim was the criticism of organised religion, and its members attacked the churches and their teachings at open-air meetings on Sunday afternoons. It is difficult for us to imagine the street culture of politics a century ago; with little bar kirk and pub to entertain them, people flocked to open-air meetings of religious revivalists, temperance campaigners and political agitators, often for the entertainment value. The two most popular open-air stances in the Shaws were Shawbrig itself, and the Old Town House, whose steeple still remains today. Hundreds came to listen and to heckle at these meetings. These meetings were covered in the *Pollokshaws News,* which reported in 1901 that Maclean had said socialism would reduce drunkeness, 'and the diminution of drunkenness would result in the diminution of crime'. A lively correspondence ensued from these coverages, to which Maclean himself contributed. Friend and foe alike agreed that Maclean was an electrifying speaker.

The Labour Representation Committee (LRC – soon to become the Labour Party) had just been formed as a federation of trades unions, Co-ops and socialist organisations. The most leftwing of the latter was the Social Democratic Federation (SDF), which was avowedly Marxist and which Maclean joined in 1903, setting up the Pollokshaws branch at an open-air meeting outside the Old Burgh Hall in 1906. Local members established a broadsheet, *The Pollokshaws Review,* which was widely distributed, and also distributed leaflets and held many street-corner meetings. The branch had about 100 members: 'Not bad for a small town,' commented Maclean. Lecturers from outside were invited, speaking at the new Burgh Hall, the pride of the Shaws, designed by Rowand Anderson and erected in 1898, to whose construction costs Sir John Maxwell contributed £20,000. Here too Maclean and the SDF would gather to hear the results of their participation in local elections, which were generally disappointing. The SDF won no council seats in the Shaws or in Glasgow, though the more moderate Independent Labour Party did, preparing the way for its staggering success of gaining ten of Glasgow's fifteen parliamentary seats in 1922, with 51% of all votes cast.

Greater success was had however by the SDF with the rapidly expanding Co-operative movement. Pollokshaws Co-op lay just south of the present Library in Shawbridge Road, and more or less over the dyke of the Sir John Maxwell school – again emphasising the 'village' character of the Shaws at this time. Maclean was an active member of the Pollokshaws Co-operative Society and like others of the SDF argued for a more socialist orientation in the organisation, and he gave lectures to members organised by the Co-operative Educational Committtee. Maclean was also elected to represent The Shaws at the national Co-op conference in 1905. Another area of activity was the Eastwood School Board, for which the SDF stood candidates demanding radical education reforms, and where two SDF members were elected in 1908–9. The SDF members called for free, non-denominational education, the raising of the school leaving age to 16 and bursaries for further education.

Maclean and his comrades were also involved in the industrial disputes of the time. One of these took place in the village of Neilston, at the thread mills where hundreds of girls struck for better wages and a trades union. Some of them lived in the village of Nitshill near the Shaws, and they contacted Maclean and his associates, who gave the girls their support. A march was organised from Neilston to the manager's house at Pollokshields in Glasgow, carrying effigies of the manager to be burnt. One participant recalled:

> Maclean was equal to anything of this kind. He was full of fun and chaff, and so took the hearts of the girls that they would have done anything for him.
>
> The march with a great banging of tin cans and shouting and singing pursued its noisy way from Neilston to Pollokshields, where the respectable inhabitants were thoroughly disturbed. The meeting was held in a field adjacent to the manager's house. The wage demands were won. The whole of the girls in the factory were organized.

As a schoolteacher Maclean worked in various parts of the South Side of Glasgow; in Polmadie, in Strathbungo and in Kinning Park, but he also taught in Pollokshaws. In 1854 Sir John Maxwell, 8th Bart, had set up an industrial school in the village, training boys for useful trades. This was rebuilt in a new site at Christian Street in 1907 by a partnership between the Burgh council and Sir John Maxwell, 10th Bart – and the school was named after him. The SDF members of the School Board proposed, and got, Maclean a night-school job at the John Maxwell School.

From 1908 to 1915 (when he was sacked by the School Board from his day and evening classes for his agitation against the First World War) Maclean taught industrial history and economics at the Sir John Maxwell to classes of industrial workers, using Karl Marx's *Capital* as the main text book. Hundreds of workers passed through these classes, their fees paid by their trades unions or by local authority grants. The school still functions as the Shaws primary, and as my son attended it, I often had cause to be there. Maclean's classes must have been held in the gymnasium as no room would have been big enough for the numbers attending. A commemorative plaque would not be out of place.

Many of the shop stewards who attended Maclean's classes became prominent in the industrial unrest (Red Clydeside) during and after the First World War. What is astonishing is that the Eastwood School Board initially paid Maclean to give these classes, and that Sir John Maxwell himself was a member of the board. The village atmosphere of the Shaws at this time is further emphasised by the fact that one of Maclean's assistants at his evening classes was another Shaws boy whom he had converted to socialism, James Maxton (later MP for Bridgeton 1922–46). Maxton's own father had taught at Pollock Academy when Maclean was a pupil.

Large numbers who attended the Marxist evening classes came from the huge new industrial complex of Weir's of Cathcart, with which Maclean had an especial connection, as it lay near to the Shaws. He gave many factory-gate meetings at Weir's during strikes before and after 1914, at a time when his influence was at its greatest and his political clarity at its sharpest. William (later Lord) Weir's role with the Ministry of Munitions made him an especial target for

15

Maclean. The latter was delighted when in 1915 the first significant strike during the war broke out at the Cathcart plant, when 2,000 men downed tools. From then until the defeat of the 40-hour strike in 1919, Weir's was one of the bastions of Clydeside militancy. William Weir's attitude to the strikes was outraged jingoism, and he fulminated that 'nothing other than martial law in the munitions districts will solve our troubles and difficulties'.

From day one, Maclean denounced the war as an imperialist one and called for the workers of all countries to take action against it. This tireless message earned him both praise from Lenin and spells of imprisonment. His words from the dock in May 1918 still thrill: 'I am here, then, not as the accused,' he stated, 'I am here as the accuser of capitalism dripping with blood from head to foot'. Before this, 100,000 Clydeside workers had struck on 1 May, demanding an end to the war, and the May Day procession was rerouted past Duke Street Jail where Maclean awaited trial. The marchers chanted John's name so that he could hear even within his cell. Weir's is one of the few industrial plants from that Red Clydeside period still working today, employing 800 workers.

In 1909 Maclean had married Agnes Wood and moved to Langside, to the east of Pollokshaws. His increasingly national political profile, and then his opposition to the First World War resulting in periods of imprisonment, took him away from the Shaws. The toleration shown by the political establishment to Maclean and his views rapidly evaporated when war was declared, and he was soon fired from his teaching job. These strains led to the breakdown of his marriage. Though his wife was not overtly hostile to Maclean's politics, her family was, and she herself was not politically engaged. On his release from prison he returned to Pollokshaws, and took rooms at 42 Auldhouse Road, a short distance from where he was born, and within sight, across the River Cart, of the factories where his parents had laboured. He was hoping that this would be a base for a reconciliation with his wife, and he had the place redecorated with money he could scarcely afford, hoping vainly that he might be re-employed in a teaching post.

He kept up his frenzied level of political activity, but his health had been seriously sapped by his spells in prison. Also he relied on pamphlet sales and collections at meetings to maintain himself; with the onset of the postwar slump these sources of income dried up, and at the end Maclean was apparently living on a diet of oatmeal and dates. Characteristically, at a time when he was giving debilitating outdoor winter lectures, he gifted his only overcoat to an immigrant from Barbados, Neil Johnston, whom he had given shelter to in his house. From 42 Auldhouse Road Maclean took his last earthly trip to Eastwood cemetery. James Maxton was one of the pallbearers.

And what of the Shaws? Even in 1955, 77% of the population of Pollokshaws lived in one or two rooms, 89% had no bath and 83% of the housing was classed as substandard. The area was comprehensively flattened, leaving only a few public buildings, and replaced by 12 multistorey blocks of flats. Two things that Maclean would definitely have approved of, however, are that there are far fewer public houses in the Shaws than a century ago – and far fewer churches as well. Or rather three things. In lieu of death duties, the daughter of Sir John Maxwell left Pollok estate to the city of Glasgow, and it is now a public park, not a private estate. Maclean would have seen that as progress.

Bounded by the River Cart, a dual carriageway and the railway line, the Pollokshaws Triangle is still very much of a village, with a community feel to it. Most people know most people, and talking to them I discovered that they still know John Maclean.

Govanhill

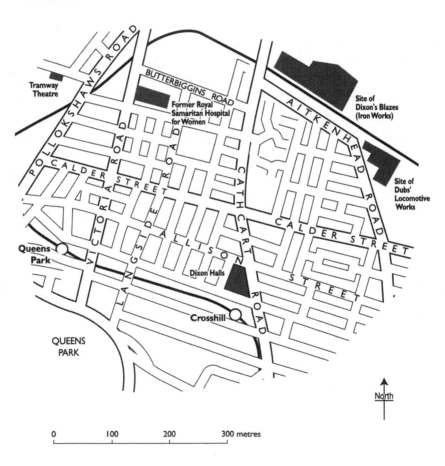

Tramway Theatre

POLLOKSHAWS ROAD

BUTTERBIGGINS ROAD

Former Royal Samaritan Hospital for Women

Site of Dixon's Blazes (Iron Works)

AITKENHEAD ROAD

Site of Dubs' Locomotive Works

CALDER STREET

VICTORIA ROAD

CALDER STREET

ALLISON STREET

LANGSIDE ROAD

CATHCART ROAD

Queens Park

Dixon Halls

STREET

Crosshill

QUEENS PARK

North

0   100   200   300 metres

CHAPTER TWO

Govanhill Retro

IF YOU WISHED to make a film depicting working-class life in Glasgow before 1914 there would be no need to establish a film set. All you would have to do would be to set it in Govanhill. No other area in the city retains so many of its Victorian and Edwardian tenements, as well as the intact street grid plan along which they were laid out. Further, Govanhill holds onto almost all its built-in civic amenities: park, hospital, library, burgh hall, churches and, until recently, baths and steamie – from a century ago.

I lived off Govanhill's Victoria Road for a couple of years when I came to Glasgow over three decades ago. One of my habitations was in Langside Road in a good working-class tenement with living room, bedroom, kitchen and bathroom – and a tiled wally close. Though I had a bath I had no washing machine so I used the steamie as well as the swimming baths, read the papers in the library and strolled in Queen's Park on fine days. There was a huge variety of shops on Allison Street: many, like the watchmaker's and shoemaker's, were still owned by Jews, and one could hear Yiddish spoken on entering. There were plenty decent pubs, and Nesson's used to deliver up the finest pint of Guinness then obtainable outside Ireland, once you waded through the cigarette ends to the bar. Separated from the Gorbals (then at its lowest ebb) by only a railway line, Govanhill was an entirely different working-class world. Govanhill was an area people wanted to live in, and is one of the few inner-city working-class districts of Glasgow which have not lost population in the last 30 years.

Govanhill was helped by the fact that its industry lay outside its residential areas, yet was readily accessible to the population. There was very little hereabouts until the early nineteenth century, when the lands of Govanhill began to be dotted with miners' rows. Many of the mines were opened after 1822 by William Dixon, the first of a dynasty of English coal and ironmasters who moved to Glasgow.

Dixon built his own primitive railway, with horse-drawn wagons, to carry his coal to the river. Using this coal, the second William Dixon opened the Govan Iron Works in 1839, on lands between Govanhill and the Gorbals. By 1842 when the factory inspector paid him a visit and left a report, Dixon employed 800 workers at this works and was one of the biggest coal and iron capitalists in the west of Scotland. The inspector also recorded Dixon's iron grip on his men, who worked a ten-hour day – or more. No membership of any unions or other organisations was allowed, and child labour was widespread. Dixon did, however, provide rudimentary schooling, a library and other cultural activities for his workers. He was an argumentative and litigious man and spent a staggering £250,000 on lawsuits, many unsuccessful, which brought the company into financial difficulties.

William 'Crimea' Simpson painted a fine watercolour of the works in the 1840s, its blast furnaces viewed from Govanhill, then still largely open spaces. Dixon's iron works became known as 'Dixon's Blazes', a commentator observing that 'the bright glare cheers a long winter's night.' But the Govanhill coal mines were soon worked out and the third William Dixon feued the land thereabouts out for housing from 1869. This led to the construction, between then and 1900, of Govanhill as it largely remains today. By 1900 the last of the old miners' 'raws' had also been demolished. For a working-class area, Govanhill had a lot of churches. The first, interestingly enough, was a Wesleyan Methodist church, probably built for the large number of English ironworkers Dixon brought from Shropshire to work at the Govan Iron Works. Govanhill became a burgh in 1871 and Dixon the Third donated Dixon Hall as its offices. But he also donated the same building to Crosshill, a middle-class development actually in Renfrewshire, which achieved burgh status at the same time. (Govanhill was in Lanarkshire). The municipal building was divided internally, and had two entrances, one for each county.

The Govanhill Library came along in 1906, one of those designed by J Rhind following the Carnegie bequest to the city, and the steamie and public baths followed before 1914. The Samaritan Hospital built 'for the care of poor women' was opened in 1903, an interesting building with lots of Art Nouveau and Arts and Crafts details in its construction. Govanhill had its own park, a small area bought by the council to prevent overbuilding, but Queen's Park, one of the city's finest, lay to the south. This was laid out by James Paxton, who designed the Crystal Palace exhibition in London. In Queen's Park many years ago I had one of those experiences hard to have outside Glasgow. I was sitting sunning myself on a bench when a Glesca character, the waur for drink, came and sat beside the two Norwegian girls on the next bench. Sensing their anxiety I decided to keep a Galahadish eye on the situation.

After a suitable pause he asked where they were from, and was told Norway and that they were holidaying in Scotland.

'Name five famous Scotsmen,' he demanded of them.

Before they could reply he rattled off a dozen or so, to the surprise of the girls, but not to me. I'd seen this Glesca floorshow before. But not the next bit, I hadn't.

'Name five famous Norwegians,' he further demanded. Astonishment rather than ignorance probably prevented the girls replying, before he said: 'Ibsen, Grieg – bit his ancestors were Scottish – Amundsen, Munch ... and Quisling, but he was a bastard and hardly coonts.'

Having achieved his desired effect he rose and walked off. You get a better class of underclass in Glasgow.

In 1868 Queen's Park FC played their first game here, and the Govanhill folk soon had both Hampden and Cathkin, home of Third Lanark, on their doorsteps. The 1920s cinema boom created no less than four cinemas in Govanhill, all of which eventually closed and were demolished apart from the one in Bank Hall Street, built in 1925. Though its interior was gutted, the tiled exterior remains, an eclectic mix of a Moorish mosque and a Hindu temple, and is appropriate to the fantasy world created by the early cinema. Further to all these delights, the good folk of Govanhill also had their own local dancehall, the Plaza at Eglinton Toll. This was for some time the only venue in once-dance-crazy Glasgow to escape closure, but has sadly now closed its doors.

The houses constructed in Govanhill were amongst the best for working people, not only in Glasgow but possibly in Britain, at this time. All the houses built had internal sanitation, very unusual then. They were also constructed to a minimum specification of two rooms, lowering the population density. In 1891 when it was annexed by Glasgow, Govanhill had a population of about 15,000; the adjacent Gorbals covered almost exactly the same surface area, and had a population of 50,000. The district managed to maintain this enviable status: in a survey of the city in 1935, less than 3% of the population was living in single ends in Govanhill, the sixth-lowest rate for any city ward – including the middle-class areas. In the period of comprehensive development in the 1960s and 70s, parts of eastern Govanhill were demolished and replaced by new housing. But the local people fought against wholesale demolition, and formed housing associations to work for the restoration of Govanhill, rather than its destruction. Later in the 1990s they waged a bitter, but unsuccessful campaign against the closure of Govanhill baths, as the council sought to centralise such facilities in newer sports complexes. Despite this loss Govanhill remains an unrivalled cameo of pre-1914 working-class Glasgow.

Railways often form social and territorial borders, and this is clear if you get out of the train at Crosshill Station. Crosshill was built as a middle-class suburb of Glasgow from the 1860s, and its grand villas and later terraces facing Queens Park were originally far from, but eventually approached by, Govanhill. Crosshill had a population of 4,000 when it was incorporated into Glasgow in 1891, dwarfed by its working-class neighbour, which you enter as soon as you drop down the hill from the station. Dixon Halls is directly in front of you, an attractive, if architecturally undistinguished, building, now serving as a day centre. East along Allison Street takes you to Aitkenhead Road, and Polmadie.

If Crosshill was Govanhill's posh satellite, then Polmadie was its underbelly, though not without its civic pride, according to the refrain:

Napoleon was the Emperor
And he ruled the land and sea
He was king o France and Germany
But he never ruled Polmadie

Napoleon never ruled Polmadie but it has its bloody history. Originally a weaving hamlet, its population were strong Covenanters.

In 1685, in the Killing Times, two weavers and a labourer from Polmadie were arrested for adherence to the Covenant and executed. Robert Thome, Thomas Cooke and John Urie are buried in Cathcart Kirk where, until recently, an annual service in remembrance was held. Their burial stone records that their captors 'murthered them with shots of guns. Scarce time did they to them allou befor their maker ther knies to bow. This cruell wickedness yow see was don in lon of Polmadie.'

Between Cathcart Road and Aitkenhead Road the housing is not of the standard further west and here is where some demolition took place. And on the far side of Aitkenhead Road is the nearest it gets in Govanhill to a ghetto. This was the less desirable end of Govanhill, as it lay next to the industrial district. Dixon's Blazes was just across the railway line at this point, with its noise and pollution, and the Caledonian Railway repair workshops were also set up here in 1879. On the Govanhill side of the railway too were several industrial units of interest. One was 'the yard where many boats were built but never one launched'. The Sentinel Works was opened in 1880. Here on Polmadie Road and Jessie Street 1,000 men prefabricated small river and lake craft which were exported and then assembled at their destinations, the lakes of Africa and Asia, and the rivers of South America.

But the most important works in Polmadie were the Queen's Park Locomotive Works, established in 1864 by the German engineer and entrepreneur Henry Dubs. Many of Glasgow's entrepreneurs came from furth the city, but few from as far as Darmstadt, where Dubs had been born. Dubs had worked in the Springburn locomotive industry, but broke out on his own. He was very successful, and soon employed 2,500 men. By his death in 1876 he had made a fortune of £120,000, and the works were producing 100 locomotives a year. Fierce competition caused Queen's Park to amalgamate with the North British Locomotive Co in 1905, and the works shared the fate of their parent when they closed in 1962 – just two years short of their centenary. Though it had a different pronunciation, Dubs' name was spelt the same as the old Scotch work for mud, and the works were known as The Dubs. That his workers may have had other problems than mud is show by the following refrain:

We're railwaymen at Polmadie
In a hotter place you couldn'a be
And when in Hell we gaither when we dee
We'll be nane the waur than in Polmadie

Just before the closure of the Queen's Park Locomotive Works, the Govan Iron Works had also shut their doors in 1959, as did most of the other industrial units in Polmadie. Today there are some ware-housing facilities, repair shops – and the council's rubbish incinerator whose huge towers dominate the skyline. Post-industrial Polmadie has replaced its industrial forebear. From Aitkenhead Road we cross Cathcart Road again, and find the delightfully named Butterbiggins Road.

That Govanhill had a pre-industrial history is shown by the name of this street, which divides a bus depot from the Royal Samaritan Hospital, now converted into housing. The name Butterbiggins Road refers to a time when there was a dairy here, and the local pop-ulation still spoke broad Scots, for biggins is the word for buildings. This street carries you onto the main thoroughfare of Govanhill, Victoria Road. This is a fine street of well-maintained sandstone ten-ements and mainly good-quality shops, ending in the heights of Queen's Park.

On Coplaw Street, across Victoria Road, there used to be a Jewish theatre where the Avron Greenbaum players put on regular and excellent dramatic performances. I attended a couple of these when I lived in Govanhill, and the audience was predominantly Jewish. Like the *Jewish Echo,* which used to be located a little north of St Andrew's Cross, this theatre has sadly gone. But Govanhill still has a theatrical life. At the end of Coplaw Street where it joins Pollokshaws Road, was located the old Corporation Tramway Works, where Glasgow's wonderful trams were constructed from 1899 onwards. This building later became the Transport Museum, and latterly has become, in the Tramway Theatre, one of the most interesting loca-tions for theatrical productions in Scotland, if not in all of Europe.

A stroll down Victoria Road leads to Allison Street. Allison Street is more *vif* and demotic than Victoria Road, and where once were Jewish shopkeepers, the shops and the neighbouring tenements are now increasingly being occupied by Glasgow's immigrant Muslim community. The Pakistanis have been a great boon to Glasgow, making it not only the curry capital of the UK, but also bringing in some welcome additions to the local genetic stock in the form of the gallus lads and gorgeous lassies of their community. Where Allison Street joins Cathcart Road, you are back at the Dixon Halls, and Crosshill station. Going back, Govanhill still seems to be a comfortable place to live. I propose it deserves recognition as a Conservation Area. Maybe that way the Govanhill folk might get their pool back.

Gorbals

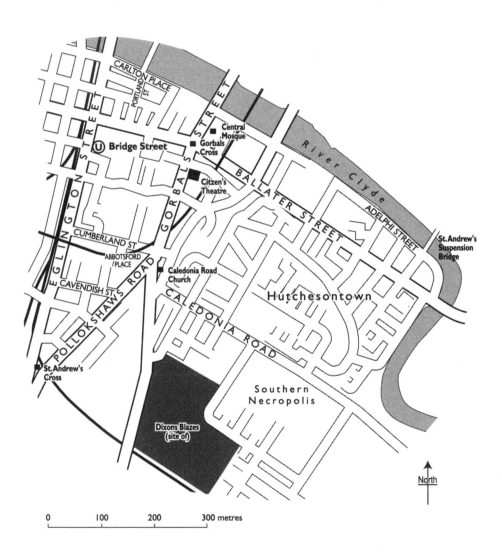

CHAPTER THREE

Gorbals: A New Glasgow Suburb

IN THE EARLY YEARS of the nineteenth century the burghers of Glasgow looked across the river and saw, adjacent to the existing village of Gorbals, a prestigious example of Regency town planning rising on the southern bank of the Clyde. The aristocratic names of its streets reflected its aspirations: Bedford, Eglinton, Norfolk. After two chequered centuries, half-way through which the Gorbals became identified as one of Europe's worst slums, the wheel is turning if not full, at least part circle, and the area is again being developed as a desirable place to live. The Gorbals of *No Mean City* and the gangster world of Jimmy Boyle is disappearing.

Emerging into daylight at Bridge Street Subway station on Eglinton Street, such an urban renaissance is not immediately apparent, as around you lie large tracts of derelict land, functioning mainly as commuter car parks. But two centuries ago this area was the site of the development of Laurieston, Glasgow's newest suburb, which the Laurie brothers hoped would make their fortune. Carlton Place, fronting the Clyde, was the jewel in the crown of this development and thankfully is fully extant today, though functioning as offices, not as the original housing. Laurieston House here was deemed grand enough to host George IV on his projected Glasgow trip of 1822 – only he never visited the city to see the interiors which had been done by the same Italian artists who decorated his own Windsor Castle. Though much of Laurieston was never built, due to the bankruptcy of the Lauries, it is a mistake to see the Gorbals area as falling immediately into universal decay.

Much quality middle-class housing continued to be erected after the Lauries' plans were abandoned, such as Abbotsford Place in the 1830s. Each dwelling here had seven or eight rooms, with a mews for the horse-carriage out back. Examination of the mid-nineteenth century censuses shows that Laurieston retained its middle-class status until well after many think, and it was only the development of the suburban railways, connected to new housing around the Queen's Park area to the south, that caused the middle classes to finally leave the area. In 1872 Tweed's *Guide to Glasgow and the Clyde* described a walk down Eglinton Street, and noted the many 'graceful buildings' in this 'fine street,' recommending to the tourist a circular walk through the area – which he would hardly have done, were it a slum. Even in the 1930s Abbotsford Place was known as the Harley Street of Glasgow, and seeing photographs of the wonderful, now-demolished buildings, would make you weep for their loss.

Heading south down Eglinton Street today is sadly not the experience it was in Tweed's time, and virtually nothing remains from that period – indeed from any but the most recent era. Passing a couple of 1930s cinemas, one disused and one restored as the highly successful Carling Academy rock-concert venue, leads you towards a landscape of derelict railway viaducts, waste ground and some examples of 1970s housing at its least imaginative. At the corner of Cavendish Street is a 1980s red-brick dwelling, admittedly better than its 70s neighbours, but a mere shadow of what it replaced. Here till 1980 stood one of the glories of Alexander 'Greek' Thomson, his Queen's Park Terrace block of middle-class tenements, constructed between 1856 and 1860. Though subsequently suffering multiple occupancy and deterioration, their demolition by Glasgow District Council was one of the greatest acts of vandalism in the city's history. Thomson, probably Glasgow and Scotland's most original nineteenth-century architect, lived in this desirable area himself, at Apsley Street from 1847–57, when he designed Queen's Park Terrace.

A little to the south Cavendish Street, where Eglinton Street – and the Gorbals – ends at St Andrews Cross, lies a row of rather scruffy shops. Here until 1992 one of the premises housed the offices of the *Jewish Echo*, Glasgow's own English-language weekly Jewish newspaper, published since 1928, when it replaced earlier Yiddish publications. As the Glasgow middle classes left Laurieston, their house became sub-let and occupied by new arrivals, amongst whom the Jews from Eastern Europe were to be the most prominent. By 1885 half the children at Gorbals Primary School were Jewish. The community – about 10,000 souls – was large enough to support the building of a synagogue in South Portland Street, the establishment of a Talmud Torah school and a Zionist reading room. But organisations which integrated the Jews into Glasgow life were also founded, such as the Oxford Star football team, and the Jewish Lads Brigade, which boasted the only all-Jewish pipe band in the world. Green's Kosher Hotel in Abbotsford Place was a point of arrival or transit for many Jews fleeing persecution first from Czarist Russia and then from Nazi Germany. Glasgow Council organised meetings in 1892 to protest against persecution of the Jews in Russia, and in 1933 boycotted German goods in protest against Hitler's anti-Semitism. Many of the Jews worked in the sweated trades and were active in the early trades union and socialist movement, like 'Manny' Shinwell, Glasgow's adoptive Jew and Red Clydesider. Others, like Isaac Woolfson, made their mark on the business world – or in the arts, such as the sculptor Benno Schotz.

A fascinating picture of Jewish life in the Gorbals is given in Ralph Glasser's *Growing up in the Gorbals*. The son of a Jewish immigrant, Glasser worked in the textile trade before winning a scholarship to Oxford. His book describes the Gorbals of the 30s

Swann's *Views of Glasgow*, plate 20. *Carlton Place from Clyde Street.*
The Regency splendour of the Laurie Brothers' Gorbals
development – and sheep grazing on the riverbanks!
Glasgow City Council (Museums)

with its gangs, appalling housing conditions, and unemployment. Glasser recalls coming out of school and seeing workless men waiting in hope outside Dixon's ironworks:

> Outside the twenty foot high gates were clustered a couple of dozen men in cloth caps, fustian jackets and mufflers, heavy black trousers ties with string below the knees. Lantern jawed, faces glazed with cold, collars turned up under their ears and heads bowed, they stood huddled upon themselves, sheltering as sheep do on a storm-swept hillside. These men waited on a stroke of luck, a call for extra hands.

He also contrasts the older Jewish political world with its philosophical Kropotkinite anarchism centred round the cosy stove and library of the Workers' Circle, with the attractions of communism to himself and the younger Jews of the period, faced with the war in Spain and Nazi anti-Semitism.

The Gorbals' reputation as a centre of political radicalism goes back earlier than the 1930s, however. John Maclean's connections with the Gorbals are many. As early as January 1918 he was appointed by the new Bolshevik government in Russia as their Consul in Scotland. At 12 Portland Street, just behind Carlton Place, Maclean set up his office. His press was censored, his Russian secretary arrested and deported, and money sent to him was blocked. Maclean sent out an appeal for financial help to labour organisations and for 'all class-conscious international workers to stand by our Russian comrades'. His work included helping political refugees get back to Russia after the Revolution of 1917. He also organised help for the dependants of the Russian and Lithuanian coal miners in Lanarkshire. These men, not British citizens, had been forcibly enlisted in the Russian army by Britain in 1917 and their families were destitute.

In the period after World War One, John Maclean's work had an especial focus on the Gorbals, where he stood twice for parliament. In 1918 he was endorsed by the anti-war Gorbals Labour Party – the British Socialist Party to which Maclean now belonged had re-affiliated to Labour. He stood against a pro-war candidate supported and enforced by the Labour Party nationally; Maclean got 7,500 votes against 14,000 for the pro-war Barnes. He stood again as an independent communist in 1922, campaigning for a Scottish Workers' Republic, and by this time he was being aided in his Gorbals and other work by Harry McShane. Though defeated he polled a respectable number of votes, over 4,000 in 1922 against the ILP candidate.

But this was the period of Maclean's political decline, when he made a series of disastrous errors. Firstly he stood aloof from the newly formed Communist Party, and secondly he emphasised more and more Scottish independence, misinspired by events in Ireland. Maclean's integrity can never be faulted, but in the years after 1919 his political judgement increasingly has to be. For example he was convinced that Britain would soon go to war with the USA, and such a conviction informed many of his political actions.Though still personally revered, he was increasingly politically isolated, and even his loyal lieutenant Harry McShane abandoned Maclean for the Communist Party.

In his autobiography, *No Mean Fighter*, McShane observes:

We had conducted the best propaganda and agitation in the West of Scotland, but we had left no organisation behind us. I knew I had to join an organisation. I joined the Communist Party in 1922. This meant a complete break with John Maclean.

The next year McShane was being evicted from his house in the Gorbals, and a large crowd gathered to contest the eviction. Another crowd came to give their support, led by Maclean, but they didn't speak. Poignantly, McShane states, 'We looked at each other, saw each other, and I never saw him again'.

At the gushet of St Andrews Cross, Pollokshaws Road leads back north towards the Gorbals, passing the fine old Abbotsford School (up for sale) on our left, set amidst piecemeal housing development and land that has lain derelict for over 30 years. Ariving at Gorbals Street, we enter territory with a much more ancient pedigree than Laurieston, which we have just walked through. The Gorbals has medieval origins, and was at one time Glasgow's leper colony. It grew to a population of 5,000 by 1800, and had swelled to 36,000 by the time it was annexed by Glasgow in 1846. At this time Gorbals Cross was still a cluster of buildings, many dating from the seventeenth century. But the old baronial dwellings had been subdivided into festering slums and the back lands were breeding grounds of squalor. This situation worsened when Gorbals became one of the favoured settlement areas for the impoverished Irish immigrants who poured into Scotland from the 1840s. One observer commented in the 1850s:

> We are really grieved to part with some of these old landmarks of the city, and we cannot help urging the proprietors of such houses as exist to pay some little attention to them, and above all to prevent them falling prey to the hordes of Irish immigrants who have a fancy to burrow in these ancient spots.

But those which did not fall into ruin were swept away by the City Improvement Trust from the 1870s, and by 1900 the area around Gorbals Street was entirely tenemented. The amazing thing is that this Gorbals too has almost totally vanished in its turn. On Gorbals Street remains one empty and derelict tenement, James Salmon II's fine British Linen Bank, and nothing else, except at its southern end a pub which brazenly states its alleigance to Celtic FC (unsurprising given the fact that Celtic greats Pat Crerand and Charlie Gallacher hailed from the Gorbals, though its most famous sporting son was the boxer Benny Lynch, now commemorated in Benny Lynch Court in Hutchesontown). Here too is found the Citizens Theatre, which has had its exterior in the form of a set of statues, moved inside for safe keeping. The 'Citz' was originally the Princess' Theatre, more in the music-hall tradition, till it was taken over by James Bridie, the playright, in 1945. Under the now-departed Giles Havergal it became one of Europe's most renowned theatre companies.

To the north of the Citz, across what once was Gorbals Cross and is now a windy, littered set of traffic lights, lies the Glasgow Central Mosque. Though you will see few Asian faces in the Gorbals today, it was initially the main area of Asian settlement in Scotland, with up to 10,000 living there, and it even boasted a newspaper, *The Young Muslim*. When the tenements were demolished the Asians had little claim on, or desire to live in, the new council housing, and, like the Jews before them, moved out. Nevertheless, the new mosque was built here and opened in 1984. One inadvertant side-effect of redevelopment in the Gorbals has been to turn what was once Glasgow's most multi-racial inner-city area into what is now probably its least.

From the former Gorbals Cross, Ballater Street leads into Hutchesontown. Although this too was begun as a prestige development, it appears to have gone down market long before Laurieston, despite its facing Glasgow Green. Possibly the opening of Dixon's Blazes iron works in 1839 on the southern edge of Hutchesontown, on the site of Dixon's existing coal mines, had something to do with this. We should remember, however, that the Victorians didn't have our anti-industrial bias, and indeed Dixon's Blazes was something of a tourist attraction. Tweed comments in his *Guide to Glasgow and the Clyde* in 1872 that:

> The stranger who wishes to see in full operation one of the most extensive and important of local industries, should spend an hour or two in visiting the works, admission to which will readily be granted on application.

Certainly Hutchesontown became much more industrialised than Laurieston, with low-paid unskilled and semi-skilled work predominating. (Dixon's higher-paid workers lived in Govanhill, an area of better-quality working-class housing to the south of the Blazes.) By 1900 this poverty, allied to overcrowding which was phenomenal even by Glasgow standards, meant that the area had infant mortality and premature death rates many times the city average. Even in 1951, the Gorbals had a population of 50,000 crowded into what one writer described as the area of an average dairy farm.

The Hutchesontown area was carpetbombed by the developments in the 1960s and 70s, and there was hardly a single historical building left standing. Little more than the odd public building – such as the public library, and the predominantly Catholic churches (for this was the heart of Glasgow's Irish community) – remained amidst the tower blocks erected at that time. The old tenements were replaced by experiments in social engineering which were of limited success. The notorious 'Hutchie E' maze of precast concrete wind tunnels was rendered rubble as early as 1987, while the knighthood-winning Basil Spence's Queen Elizabeth Court tower blocks followed in 1993. In consequence the population of the Gorbals had been reduced to 10,000 by 2001 – 20% of what it had been half a century before. It is Hutchesontown which is undergoing the most intensive redevelopment of mixed housing association and private housing, and walking around the area is an uplifting experience, showing off the advantages of coherent and human-scale town planning. There is even a new hotel in the area, taking advantage of the Gorbals' proximity to the town centre.

It is worth taking a sidetrail off Ballater Street to Adelphi Street and the St Andrews Suspension Bridge over the Clyde; amongst the tree lined river banks one could almost imagine oneself by the Seine. Crossing Ballater Street again into McNeill Street there lies a mix of renovated and newly built housing, with imaginative street furniture. The remaining high-rise blocks here (not everyone hated the high life) are being reclad to soften their look and blend with the new buildings. You can wander for ages around Hutchesontown with profit, but eventually you should emerge onto Caledonia Road, beside the Southern Necropolis, which thankfully appears to be getting better maintenance than formerly. Here in lair 3971 lies the vault of Thomas Lipton, the Gorbals boy, born of poor Irish immigrant parents, who became a millionaire by the time he was 30 with his chain of grocery shops.

Glasgow Fair 1835 from the Courthouse roof.
The scene of demotic abandon which was the fair at its height.
Stalls, shows, penny-geggies, drink, romance, fights...
Glasgow City Council (Museums)

On the north side of Caledonia Road are found some of the larger new houses, built in a stunning style that gives the lie to those who think modern architecture is worthless; these buildings would grace any European city. Across from them, next to the Necropolis, is the site of Dixon's Blazes, closed in 1962, now a rather unlovely trading estate. But just adjacent, like something out of Athens or Rome, stands the shell of Alexander Thomson's Caledonia Road Church (the tenements he built flanking it are long gone). When this church lost its congregation, it was bought by Glasgow Council with a view to restoration. This never took place, and instead the building became a target for vandals, and now all that remains are the walls and spire. So little survives in the Gorbals of the historical environment that the salvation of this church must be a priority: indeed, given Thomson's status, it must be a national and international priority. This will give Glasgow Council the chance to atone for its other Thomson sins, and the church could be the focal point of the new Gorbals itself, as regeneration spreads westwards from Hutchesontown towards central Gorbals and Laurieston.

Walking along Cumberland Street, however, there is little sign of this, and we are back in the planning blight of the 1970s. There is not a single house in this part of the former bustling thoroughfare although the ruined former railway station remains. The abolition of the street was probably the greatest crime of 60s and 70s redevelopment: its rediscovery a main virtue of new architecture. At the end of Cumberland Street we are back on Eglinton Street, and once again near to the subway – or one can walk a little further to Carlton Place, and view Laurieston House. Crossing the river by the suspension bridge reminds you that, however hard life was in the Gorbals, it was always only ten minutes from the city centre, and ten minutes from the Green. And maybe this time, after Regency suburb, Victorian tenement slum and concrete jungle, the planners have got it right in the Gorbals.

Govan

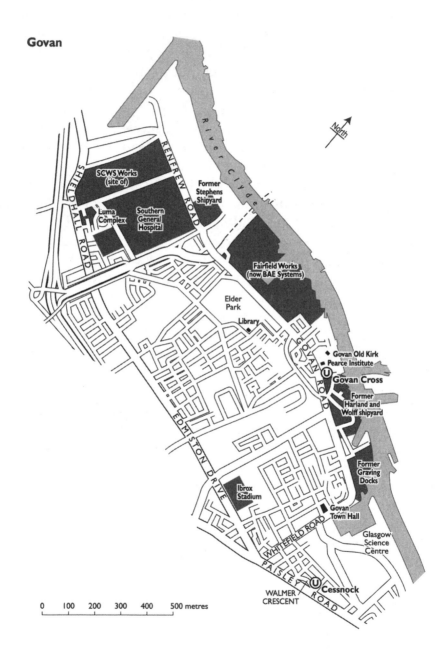

River Clyde

North

SHIELDHALL ROAD

RENFREW ROAD

SCWS Works (site of)

Former Stephens Shipyard

Luma Complex

Southern General Hospital

Fairfield Works (now BAE Systems)

Elder Park

Library

GOVAN ROAD

Govan Old Kirk
Pearce Institute
Govan Cross

Former Harland and Wolff shipyard

EDMISTON DRIVE

Ibrox Stadium

Former Graving Docks

Govan Town Hall

Glasgow Science Centre

WHITEFIELD ROAD

PAISLEY ROAD

Cessnock

WALMER CRESCENT

0   100   200   300   400   500 metres

CHAPTER FOUR

The Glories of Govan

READERS NOTING THE title of this section of the urban exploration of the Dear Green Place might think that I could only be referring to the footballing exploits of Rangers FC – familiar as they might be with the picture of Govan drawn by the string-vested philosopher Rab C Nesbit, as a place not of glory but of inner-city decay and drunks in Wine Alley. Rest assured, readers, that as an Aberdeen supporter Govan's glories for me have nothing to do with Ibrox Stadium, magnificent though its architecturally B-listed South Stand might be, and that, though Rab does describe with humour an aspect of Govan life that is really no laughing matter, there is far more to Govan than is shown in his philosophy. It has to be admitted here that Ibrox (and Parkhead) saw some of the best afternoons of my life. In the 1980s, with utter regularity, Aberdeen FC would come to Glasgow and hammer the Old Firm. The greatest moment was when my old primary-school teammate, Jocky Scott, scored three in a 5–1 gubbing of the 'Gers. But those days, like Govan's industry, will probably not return.

Where to begin, and convince you quickly of my argument? Nowhere better than by jumping on Glasgow's Clockwork Orange subway at any point and emerging – where sadly few but locals do – at Cessnock Station. Immediately on exiting you notice the unusual iron work and motifs of the station's entry arch; look at the tenement above the station, in whose bowels on Walmer Crescent the subway was tunnelled, and you will see that the station arch is echoing the motifs round the doorways of the building. When it opened in the 1890s to link Govan with the West End and City Centre, the builders of the subway were paying tribute to the genius of the architect of Walmer Crescent, which was built by Alexander 'Greek' Thomson in 1857. Though it is on the official Thomson Heritage Trail, few people come to see it as they do his city centre and suburban buildings, because of its location – and, sadly, condition. The Crescent consists of flyblown hotels and multiple occupancies – where the flats are not vacant and derelict. Yet a dentist's surgery allowed me entry to see Thomson's interior plasterwork, stencilling and woodwork. These features are on a modest scale compared to some of his buildings, for this was a crescent (i.e. flats) not a terrace (i.e. a storied house). Originally standing alone in open countryside, it housed respectable families of professionals and small businessmen, before it declined to slum status. Set back from Paisley Road, the Crescent is fronted by a promenade of shops, now sadly also in disrepair and reflecting, in the wares on sale, the poverty of the local inhabitants. Unless something is done soon, this building will go the way of Thomson's other wonderful tenement, the Gorbals' Queen's Park Terrace, which was demolished in the 1980s. Visit Walmer Crescent, publicise its plight: save it.

West from Walmer Crescent, Paisley Road West – 'the PR' as it is locally known – leads you to Whitefield Road, which in turn joins the Govan Road at Govan Town Hall. This grand building had a rather short life, being opened in 1901, to replace the earlier town hall, and operating as burgh headquarters for a mere 11 years till its functions were transferred to George Square in 1912. Around the main entrance are busts of the local dignitaries of this period, while inside is a mosaic on the floor showing Govan's equally shortlived coat of arms, and motto *Nihil Sine Labore* (Nothing without labour) – a slogan that reflects Govan's days of shipbuilding glory. Today the *umquile* Town Hall houses Glasgow Social Work Department. The former Govan graving docks lie a short distance on from the Burgh Hall. Here the Clyde-built ships were repaired and repainted for over a century. On its closure in 1988 the docks area gradually became a wasteland of ruins. However, there are plans to turn the derelict docks into an upmarket housing development, a 'little Amsterdam' of flats, a hotel and floating restaurants. The ground has recently been cleared and awaits construction work. This would be a wonderful place to live, facing onto Glasgow's futuristic Science Centre. Hopefully more will come of this idea than came of the plan for a Clyde maritime museum in the adjacent West Quay; this was scuppered when, amongst other things, the Clyde-built *Canberra* (which was supposed to be a star attraction) was instead, inexplicably and unjustifiably, located in Leith! Piracy – if not on the high seas, at least in high places.

Most people would – if they ever got there – hurry along Govan road to Govan Cross, probably in their cars. And it is true there is a lot of dereliction: empty buildings and waste ground where, behind advertising hoardings, groups of men sit drinking by fires. But they mind their business as I mind mine, and there is here so much to see; you have to be selective. Few of the tenements survive on the Govan Road, but one that does draws the eye, the Cossar building, known after John Cossar who built it to house his printing works. He moved here in 1890 after successfully establishing himself as the publisher of the *Govan Chronicle* in 1875, followed by the *Govan Press* in 1878. There are busts on the building of Burns and Scott, Scotland's two greatest writers, and of the founders of printing, Caxton and Gutenberg – and, just so that the big capitalists of the shipyards didn't have a monopoly of immortalising themselves, busts of Mr and Mrs Cossar as well. The firm closed down in 1983, as the rest of Govan's economy contracted with the collapse of shipbuilding. Cossar published TCF Brotchie's *The History of Govan* in 1905, when the area was at its peak. Brotchie commented that nowhere in Govan were you out of the sound of a hammer. In 2005 most of them are silent.

Further along on the right is Napier House, built in the Art Nouveau Glasgow style in 1899. It was one of the earliest steel-framed buildings in the city, and the top floor was also Glasgow's first telephone exchange. Formerly used as a seamen's lodging house, its occupants now are only doos which fly in and out of the broken windows. The building is not beyond repair, and viable ideas for its restoration are being sought.

By now we are at the heart of Govan, at the Cross. Two buildings especially catch the eye. One is Brechin's Bar, built in 1894 in Scots Baronial style. Ironically it was originally the centre of Govan's Temperance Movement, and was known as the Cardell Hall after its founder John Cardell. In the days when every street corner in Govan had a pub, another place you couldn't get a drink was the Pearce Institute, opened in 1906, a magnificent eclectic mix of Scottish and Dutch Renaissance architecture, with crow-step gables, oriel windows, external balconies, and a fully-rigged sailing ship (constructed by workers in the Fairfield yard.) Built by Rowand Anderson, the Institute was endowed by Lady Pearce in memory of her husband, a prime mover in the Fairfields shipbuilding yard. With its theatre, reading room and library, dining and recreation rooms, the Institute played a role in Govan social life till its sad closure a couple of years back; lack of funds has since deprived many community and voluntary groups of a venue. However, on the centenary of the beginnings of its construction in 1903, the Pearce Institute Regeneration Plan was launched. Already some vital repairs have been done on the roof and broken windows of the building with a £100,000 grant from Community Scotland – and its prominent clock is now working again. The interior of the building is basically sound, having undergone a lot of repair work about ten years ago. A large range of groups have already made the Pearce their home, including a couple of film companies and a wide variety of social and voluntary organisations.

As a charity the Pearce Institute is driven to maximise usage of its space to increase its income, though funding has also been gained from Historic Scotland and other sources. A feasibility study is underway into the establishment of a healthy-food café in the building. Tommy Docherty, a member of the Pearce Institute management group is enthusiastic:

> The Pearce Institute has been at the heart of the community in Govan since 1902. And I am confident that our action plan will play a part in bringing it back into the community as a vibrant, fully functioning, financially viable asset for everyone in Greater Govan.

In an attempt to do just this, the Institute hosted an exhibition in June 2004, illustrating various proposals for the restoration of eight historic buildings within Govan, and asking for the opinions of the local community, a community which in the past has been more planned against than planning.

Opposite the Institute is the statue known as the Black Man for its colouring; it depicts Pearce himself, who became Govan's first MP in 1885 – as a Conservative. Hailing from Kent, he moved to the Clyde from the naval dockyards at Chatham in the 1860s and by 1869 was the sole proprietor of Fairfields, becoming a millionaire before his death in 1888. Pearce will doubtless be keeping a watchful eye on the progress of the restoration of the PI. Local legend has it that the Black

Muirhead Bone *Glasgow; Fifty Drawings* (1911)
Smiths' workshop, Fairfields
A fine study of a shop in the yard at the height of its industrial power,
when 'nowhere in Govan were you out of the sound of a hammer'.
Glasgow City Council (Museums)

Man does indeed look around to see what is happening in Govan – or at least that's what the regulars at Brechin's Bar insist, usually around closing time.

The election of Pearce, the biggest local employer, as Govan's first MP illustrates an aspect of nineteenth-century life, the almost feudal power local capitalists wielded, albeit a democratic feudalism. Pearce was not unusual: many capitalists in Glasgow and elsewhere became local MPs – local provosts, councillors and JPs. Though only about half of working-class males had the vote before 1918 in national elections (more had the vote in local elections), in Glasgow as elsewhere, it was not uncommon for many of these men to vote for their employers. In a working-class area like Govan, Pearce must have been carried to Westminster largely on skilled workers' votes, and in 1910 when Labour first stood in Govan, they came third. Govan, however, was one of the places where change began to be effected, and was an early Labour Party gain. It was the only Glasgow seat which the party

won at the Khaki Election landslide of 1918, and was retained for the
ILP by Neil Maclean thereafter. Even at the next Labour wipe-out in
1931, Govan stayed with the ILP – though only by 600 votes.

When it was annexed by Glasgow in 1912, Govan was Scotland's
fifth-biggest burgh with a population of over 100,000; yet in the 1830s
the population had been only 2,000. The growth, virtually unparalleled
anywhere else in Scotland, was due almost entirely to Govan becoming
the centre of the Scottish, British and indeed world, shipbuilding industry. Robert Napier opened his works in 1841, and was followed by
John Elder, who in 1864 laid out his yard on the Fairfield farm, and he
in turn was followed by others, such as Alexander Stephen at
Linthouse. These yards built the Cunard liners and Atlantic cargo ships
as well as warships. The long decline of the industry – which featured
the famous Upper Clyde Shipbuilders work-in of the 1970s when
workers occupied the yards – led to the closing of most of the sites. But
the Fairfield works – after going through as many name changes as a
nuclear power station – survives today as BAE Sytems, employing
about, 1000 men, a shadow of its former self. At its wartime height,
the shipbuilding industry in Govan employed 50,000.

Wages were high in the shipyards – at least for skilled men – but
the working conditions were hard and dangerous. Housing – often
put up by the employers – was generally squalid and overcrowded to
a level we would find incredible today – and it was no accident that it
was in Govan that the housewives precipitated the Rent Strikes during the 1914–18 war. On the other hand the paternalism of the
Victorian employers was manifested in various ways. As well as the
Pearce Institute mentioned, the Elder Park, which lies further along
the Govan Road from the Pearce, was donated to the people of
Govan in 1885 by Mrs Isabella Elder as a memorial to her husband.
His statue (and hers) stands in the park. Elder rests his hand on the
compound steam engine he developed and patented, which with its
vast fuel savings gave the Clyde yards their competitive edge in
Victorian times. Isabella also gave money to build the Elder Cottage
Hospital and the Elderpark Library, opened by Andrew Carnegie in
1903. Inside the library are busts of John and Isabella Elder, remind-
ing us that, as well as wealth, they sought immortality. Even streets in
Govan bear the shipping magnates' names: Elder, Napier. Such pater-

nalism immortalised its practitioners, but also provided social control; reading materials in these institutions was censored to choose materials 'edifying to the working classes' and only activities approved by the patrons could take place therein.

Opposite the Elder Park the men who were really Govan's greatest benefactors are commemorated in the statues at the entrance to Fairfields. These are a duo of anonymous shipyard workers carved in sandstone by Pittendrigh MacGillivray, an Aberdeen sculptor who did much work in Glasgow. MacGillivray was an early socialist, if of a somewhat eccentric nature, and clearly sympathised with his subject. He attended meetings of William Morris' Socialist League in Glasgow in the 1880s. The *Shipwright* and *Engineer* are real-life manual workers, a break with Victorian habits of representing the trades by idealised classical maidens, cherubs or, at best, workers in the garb of medieval trades. The figures express the pride and confidence of the skilled and educated working men who were Govan's backbone for 150 years. MacGillivray was paid £250 for the work in 1890. The only other comparable work I know of is Lavery's *Shipbuilders* in the City Council Chambers, where a fine mural shows men at work in a shipyard c. 1888. This was a one-off for Lavery, a society painter whose subjects were usually a world away from working-class life, and was a commission for the council.

In *Glasgow in 1901*, written for the Glasgow exhibition of that year, its composite author James Hamilton Muir draws a picture of the Glasgow working man, and sets him in Govan. He is called John MacMillan, a fitter, and seen as the new working man, interested in football and a Rangers supporter. 'The best you can say for football is that it has given the working man a topic for conversation,' state the authors, for their imaginary typical worker is non-political. He lives in a room and kitchen and goes 'doon the watter' for his holidays:

> When his time was served he became a Union man, and thought all the world of his district delegate. He stauns up for himsel, not only against the common enemy, his employer, but also against his comrades in the allied trades if they invade his frontiers.

Despite being rather a caricature, there is a truth in this picture, as in most caricatures – a picture of what Lenin would have described as 'trades union consciousness'. Against this the authors draw a cameo of the minority of workers, whom they call the backbone of the working class, and describe them as 'radical and Calvinist by inheritance and tradition'. This type of worker ignores football and is teetotal, and 'his discussions are political and theological ... and though his active interest in Calvinism may have abated, its principles still control his conduct.'

Here we have the working class-minority, some of whom would become leaders of Red Clydeside, with the John MacMillans following them for their own economic aims, and some of whom would add a more Orange colour to the waters of the proletarian river.

It is fitting that with their rich history, the Govan yards would feature prominently in one of the last great battles of the Glasgow industrial working class, the Upper Clyde Shipbuilders' (UCS) work-in of the early 1970s. The UCS campaign led to the biggest explosion of class struggle in Glasgow since the days of Red Clydeside. The decision of the Heath government to withhold credits for yards that had full order books led to a work-in, organised mainly by shop stewards influenced by the Communist Party, and centred on Govan. Against those who argued that the UCS work-in could be a catalyst for a general strike to bring down the government, the shop stewards' committee waged a broad and moderate campaign, which drew widespread sympathy. In June 1971 100,000 people struck work in support of the workers occupying their yards, and 40,000 demonstrated in George Square; in August the numbers of those taking industrial action reached 200,000 – and 80,000, the biggest demonstration in Glasgow for over 50 years, took to the streets. Faced with this the government partially backed down, and a compromise was eventually reached, which maintained 8,500 jobs. Those who had expected the revolution were disappointed. As one worker replied to a speaker arguing for a general strike, 'That's no in ma union rule book'. When told that a simple work-in would lead to defeat the worker replied, 'Defeat? Ah'm used tae that son. Ah'm a Partick Thistle supporter'.

We have missed out something, one of Govan's greatest glories, about which few in Glasgow are aware, despite its world-historic significance. When getting to know Glasgow on foot 30 years ago, I entered the graveyard of Govan Old Parish Church to look at the gravestones, dating back to the 17th century, and to pre-industrial Govan. Finding the building open, I went in, and found that the best was actually inside. I discovered that there had been a Christian church here from at least the sixth century, well before Glasgow Cathedral was built, and that the present kirk, designed by Rowand Anderson (of the Pearce Institute) was at least the fourth to be built on the site. The history of the kirk since the Reformation throws up, amongst others, the figures of Andrew Melville (1577–80), architect of the presbyterian structure of the Church of Scotland and George Macleod (1930–8), whose experiences of Govan in the depression helped him to found the Iona Community dedicated to world peace and justice.

But even more remarkable are the collection of carved stones in the kirk, one of the most important collections of early Christian sculpture in Scotland. These were all carved locally from sandstone by skilled Govan crafstsmen, showing that, 1,000 years before the glories of shipbuilding, Govan had another glory period as a wealthy community. Amongst the sculptures, around 30 in all, are the stunning hogback burial stones, possibly from the tenth century and of Norse origin, many burial slabs and shafts combining Christian and pre-Christian motifs, and most amazing of all, the carved stone Govan Sarcophagus. This was originally assumed to be the burial coffin of St Constantine, but is now thought to be of a later date. One fascinating feature of this is the hole in the base, which allowed the decomposing matter from the body to drain out of the coffin.

Still hosting a small congregation, the Old Parish Kirk has managed to get some help to maintain and publicise its treasures. Monies have come from Historic Scotland, and Glasgow University and the Channel Four Time Team have carried out excavations. But I was saddened when a kirk elder told me that in an average year this site gets a mere 600 visitors; hopefully their new website (www.govanold.org.uk) and publicity materials will boost this number severalfold. Any Glasgwegian who has not visited here should be ashamed of themselves, and any visitor to the city should head for Govan to see the most interesting ecclesiastical building in Glasgow.

A fitting addition to any Govan perambulation is a trip west along the Renfrew Road to the site of the former SCWS complex at

Shieldhall. Many Govanites worked till its closure in this, one of the largest industrial concerns in Glasgow. At its height 6,000 people turned out footwear, furniture and foodstuffs in a whole village of factories for the chain of Co-op retail stores throughout Glasgow and Scotland. In the space left derelict since its closure, a modern village could easily be built. John Hume in his excellent *Industrial Archeology of Glasgow* is a bit sniffy about the SCWS site, saying that 'the buildings are mainly distinguished by their number'. Actually they include one of the finest industrial buildings in Glasgow. The Luma Co-op lightbulb factory, now converted to offices and flats, is a splendid art-deco sight as one enters Glasgow from the motorway on the west. If you actually go and visit the factory, you will find behind it a cluster of art-deco cottages, built by the Co-op for their workers.

The Co-op was probably the most important organisation in working-class life till the 1950s. Many more were members of the Co-op than of political parties or even of trades unions. Roughly half of Glasgow's population were Co-op members between the wars (it used to be said that when the revolution came, you would be spared if you could remember your Co-op number). The Co-op provided cheaper staples of life for working-class people, the possibility of credit at non-usurious rates, and the divvi which financed luxury purchases. The Co-op also provided employment, not only at Shieldhall but in its mass of outlet stores, in good conditions. Further, for a lucky few, it provided good housing above its tenement premises, or at Shieldhall. Working-class loyalty to the Co-ops was intense if occasionally irreverent:

I like a sassidge, a Coperative sassidge
Though ye cannae get near it for the smell
If ye fry it wi an ingan, ye'll hear the ingan singan
'Mary ma Scots Blue Belle'

The factory is reached by going along Renfrew Road past the Sufferin (Southern) General Hospital, after passing the site of the former Stephen's shipyard, now partly occupied by Barr and Stoud Optics, one of Glasgow's industrial success stories. Walking down Bogmoor Road gives you an impression of the immensity of these works, and the Luma factory with its cottages – the only relics of this once-mighty effort at economic Co-operation – is found at the head of Hardgate Road. John Maclean was active in the Co-operative movement which he saw both as a school for socialism and as a method of waging the class struggle. He foresaw the expansion of Co-operative production alongside the increasing concentration of capitalist concerns and argued to the Scottish Co-operative Conference in 1911 that:

> Working men's Co-operation is within sight of a desperate struggle with capitalists' trusts. When the ultimate struggle between the huge trusts and Co-operation takes place, it will be a fight between capital and labour.

Sadly, the capitalist trusts won.

A fitting end to a visit to Govan is to stroll to the Elderpark Library where the Govan Heritage Exhibition will elaborate on some of the things you have seen and point to others you may have missed. (Check on opening hours: 0141 445 1047). Then it is a short walk to the Govan Cross Underground and transport back to wherever you started from – or, as I usually do, you can retrace the walk back to Cessnock for just one more look at, and possibly to finally get that perfect photograph of, Walmer Crescent. People who value their heritage value their communities and also themselves. And the folk of Govan still do value their heritage, despite the economic ravages which have beset the area in the last 25 years. Who, even in Glasgow, knows that the city's oldest procession is the Govan Fair, established by Govan's weavers in 1756? (Glasgow People's Palace, by the way, hosts a banner borne by the Govan Weavers when they fought at Sheriffmuir against the Jacobites in 1715). Every year in June thousands line the streets to watch as the Govan Queen proceeds through the 'burgh', preceded by the Glasgow Police Pipe Band, two mounted policemen, and the whole parade headed by a bearer, traditionally a ship's joiner, bearing a sheep's heid. The sheep's heid represents the story of when a Govan minister forbade his servant girl from marrying a local lad; the lad eloped with the girl and decapitated all the minister's sheep into the bargain. The day of the Govan Fair is also marked by various well-supported sporting and other events. While there are ghettoes in Govan that would make a grown man weep, there is much more to Govan than Rab C and the Rangers.

Clydebank

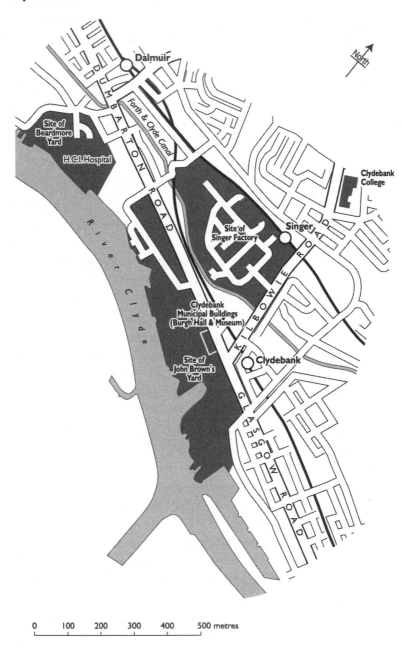

CHAPTER FIVE

Clydebank: A Cut Above

THERE ARE PLACES adjoining Glasgow which are not Glasgow. Paisley is an example. With their 800-year independent history the Buddies are not Glasgwegians. They have a different culture, expressing itself in things like a softer humour than Glasgow's – and a proverbial meanness. On the other hand there are places bordering the city which, despite the fact that Glasgow's boundaries exclude them, are in every respect Glasgwegian – and one of them is Clydebank. It is even surrounded by Glasgow, except to the west, and if ever the boundaries of the conurbation are redrawn logically, it will be a part of the city.

I worked in Clydebank at the Technical College for 22 years, teaching history. Before I got the job I knew nothing of the town, though I remembered reading an article about the place in the *Guardian* at the time of the UCS work-in of 1971–2. This was to the effect that places like Clydebank, with their nineteenth-century industries and slums, had no place in modern Britain. Never let the truth (for example that for most of the nineteenth-century Clydebank didn't even exist) stand in the way of good newspaper copy. The writer did not actually advocate bringing back the Luftwaffe to finish the job Hitler started in the 1940s, but clearly supported the then Conservative government's policy of killing so-called lame ducks – as they saw shipbuilding. But the town didn't just produce ships, it produced people. And it didn't want to disappear, either.

The best way to start a daunder round Clydebank is to do what I did many times for 22 years, and to take the train from Glasgow to Singer station. This used to be Kilbowie station and was renamed when the American Singer sewing-machine company moved its factory here from Bridgeton in Glasgow in the 1880s. By 1890 Singer's employed 6,000 people at what was one of the largest factories in the world. A siding was built off Singer station to take the special trains which carried thousands of workers from Glasgow to Singer's daily, though many families moved west with the factory. At the college I taught everything from 17-year-olds to 70-year-olds. One of the latter told me his grandfather had moved to Clydebank from Bridgeton with Singer's. The high point of Singer's was in the 1950s, when with 17,000 workers it was still the largest industrial unit in Europe. Even in the 70s when I went to Clydebank, Singer's employed 6,500 people.

Singer's was one of the first factories to apply mass-production techniques, described by John Maclean, in 1911, in *Justice*, the national paper of the Social Democratic Federation:

> There are 41 departments and the various processes have been so divided and sub divided that few outside the office staff will know how many stages the wood, iron and steel have to go through before the machine is completed. All except a few engineers, moulders and joiners, are tied down to work no longer skilled.

Only these skilled workers were unionised. The works saw the most important strike in the west of Scotland before the outbreak of wwi. Three thousand women at the factory came out in 1911, trying to form a trades union and looking for increased wages. They were followed by the unskilled and largely non-unionised male workers, the leading activists amongst whom belonged to the Socialist Labour Party (SLP), a Marxist group advocating industrial unionism (One Big Union).

Unfortunately the men in the engineering union, the ASE, did not come out in support and the strike was eventually defeated in the face of a management threat to sack the strikers. Maclean publicised the strike in *Justice*, in a series of articles. He stated:

> If the ranks are held unbroken, if discipline is maintained and if the committee is firm in attitude and unanimous in spirit and objective and tactics, then in the state of present trade, the trust will have, for the time being at least, to yield to the strikers.

And he blamed the ultimate defeat after two weeks on 'the lack of feeling of class solidarity'. The SLP men who had managed to get the unskilled workers out in support of the women were sacked after the strike.

If Singer's came from Glasgow to Clydebank, so too did the ship-yards. A decade or so before the Singer's move, Thomson's shipyard had left Govan and moved to the area, again bringing many of its workers with it (at first daily by paddle-steamer from Govan till their housing was constructed). Thomson's also brought the name Clydebank, which the town subsequently took from the shipyard itself. At first Thomson's built paddle-steamers, and later transat-lantic liners, such as *The City of New York*. John Brown's, the Sheffield steelmasters, took over the yard in 1899 and expanded it to build larger ships. From less than 1,000 people, Clydebank had grown to 30,000 by 1900. These two industrial units dominated employment in the town, but others from Glasgow followed, and a large part of the incoming population originated from the city. Clydebank was the East Kilbride of its day, a Glasgow overspill. Between the shipyard by the river and the Singer factory up the brae, the fields were filled with tenements. These were tight-packed and in 1936 40% of the housing was officially overcrowded, one of the highest figures in Scotland.

From the dilapidated Singer station you look out over Clydebank Business Park, which occupies the site of the former works, and this gives an idea of its vast scale. I remember coming back after the col-lege summer holiday in 1980 and looking over to the hills of Renfrew which I hadn't seen from Clydebank before. Puzzled, I realised Singer's had been demolished during the summer. The Singer Tower, with its four eight-metre-diameter clocks, once claimed to be the biggest timepieces in the world, had already gone by the time I started at the college. This was a magic clock, since from the inexhaustible metal of its hands every family in Clydebank has at least one ashtray. Another amazing Bankie fact is that it had the highest concentration of piano ownership in Britain. When the Blitz insurance claims went in, it was found that almost every close had boasted eight of them, one in each flat, though sadly all the evidence was destroyed!

The railway bounded Singer's to the north. If you walk down Kilbowie Road from the station, you come to the now reopened Forth and Clyde Canal, which was the factory's southern boundary. Reclamation and restoration has created a pleasant walk along the south bank of the canal for a bit under a mile, till it crosses with

Dumbarton Road. The canal carries on from here to Old Kilpatrick, with interesting protected wetlands and saltflats under the Erskine Bridge. Thereafter it leads in a couple of miles to its outlet at Bowling Docks, where the old berthings and custom house are well worth a visit. But let's stay with the Bankies for the moment.

This part of Clydebank is called Dalmuir and some local residents think it isn't really Clydebank. Dalmuir mainly exists because Beardmore built a shipyard here in the early 1900s. When it closed this left a huge asbestos dump in the site, uncovered. The local council seized on a proposal for a private hospital for part of the site, both to bring jobs during the mass unemployment of the 1980s, and as a way of capping the site – for which they didn't have the cash. So the UHI Hospital was built, a miracle state-of-the-art building, which was supposed to treat rich patients from the Gulf States and elsewhere.

Advertising materials offered helicopter flights from Glasgow airport to the UHI, to potential patients who were not told about the asbestos. Instead the brochures showed pictures of Loch Lomond as the hospital's (implied) location. A hotel, ironically called Beardmore's, was built for the prospective guests of these sick fat cats. Never more than a third full and surviving on NHS custom, the place was bought for the NHS in the 1990s – after having largely been paid for by public money in the first place. True to their radical traditions the Bankies fought long and hard against the private hospital, but at least now it is treating some of the people who paid for it.

For Clydebank has always been a very political place, possibly the most political in Scotland. In 1922 Davie Kirkwood was elected for the ILP, the only Red Clydesider elected from outwith the city boundaries, proving again that Clydebank is really Glasgow. And between the wars Clydebank became one of the power bases of the Communist Party, based largely on the shipyards, or on John Brown's, the daddy of them all, which at its maximum employed 10,000 workers. Turning back east along Dumbarton Road from Dalmuir you come to one end of the site of the former Brown's yard, but you have to walk a very long way, the best part of a mile, before you come to the other end of what was possibly British shipbuilding's greatest yard. Unlike the Fairfields yard in Govan, 'Broon's' management and office block was notable only for its size, and was without architectural merit. Nothing of it remains. A fine 'Head of a Shipyard Worker' sculpture was erected in 1992 opposite the former main gate of the yard.

Where does one start with this yard? Brown's built the *Lusitania*, whose sinking helped bring the USA into World War One. It built the *Queen Mary* in the 1930s, which signalled hope at a time when 50% of the town's workers were unemployed. And it built the *Queen Elizabeth II* in the booming 1960s when unemployment and capitalist crises were supposed to be things of the past. The yard was the focus of the UCS work-in, and the power base of its main spokesman Jimmy Reid, himself a Bankie. Like many of the leaders of the work-in, Reid was a member of the Communist Party, and in its aftermath stood for Parliament as a Workers' Candidate, getting a solid 5,000 votes. For a while the former Brown's yard operated, building oil rigs with a reduced work force, for various owners. The engineering side of the business continued with about 1,500 men until 1997, when closure ended 'Broon's' last link with the town.

Something I liked about Clydebank was the low profile of sectarianism, and this despite the fact that a good third of the population came from Ireland (from both sides of the fence). The solidly left wing nature of the place helped to dampen this division, and I can honestly say I never came across the problem in the college, except from one pupil, who was not from Clydebank, and who wrote an essay about Prodesens and Kafflicks full of the usual nonsense. As well as history I taught apprentices something called social studies. These were guys from the trades and factories, with many coming from the shipyards, and teaching them was really hard work, but often rewarding. And even in the general debate and banter, you could always tell the Bankies, they were just that bit sharper, that bit more informed, than the others.

Brown's was always half-hidden by the tenements along Dumbarton Road, and also by the civic buildings of the Burgh. Much as I love the Bankies, I am not going to claim their town as a Venice or Athens, or Rome of the North. In fact it is twinned with a town called Argenteuil in France, far, I imagine, from any tourist track. Clydebank's main asset is its people, rather than its buildings. But it has the usual cluster of civic buildings, attractive enough if not outstanding. These consist of the town hall, the library, the former baths and washhouse, and the Clydebank Museum, which hosts the world's largest collection of sewing machines. Singer deposited examples of their new models as they appeared, many of them things of real beauty. The model 15K (called after Kilbowie) sold 20 million up to 1962 when production ended, and everyone's mother used to have one of these finely-detailed black-cast machines, the older ones with the treadle, the newer ones electric. So if sewing machines are your religion, Clydebank is your Mecca.

In the appropriately named Agamemnon (he was a character in one of Aeschelus's plays as well as Homer's *Iliad*) Street off Dumbarton Road used to be situated the Clydebank Repertory Theatre, where many of Scotland's thespians first trod the boards, including Russel Hunter. By the time I was going there in the 70s and early 80s, the boards were distinctly spongy with the rot, the smell of which infested the building, but the performances were still good. And this place, which the *Guardian* thought ought not to exist, also produced possibly the finest (after Glasgow's Orpheus) amateur choir in the west of Scotland, the Clydebank Lyric, the selling of whose tickets was the periodic duty in the College of relatives of performers. And when the Red Army Choir or the USSR State Circus would come to town, busloads of Bankies could be guaranteed to attend. See Kulcher, see the Bankies.

But that does not end what these folk produced. John Brown's yard was not only a crucible of politics and trades unionism, but also of what was possibly Scotland's most important mountaineering club, the Creag Dhu. In the '30s Depression many workers were unemployed, and they used their time to good effect by working out means of getting to the hills and mountains around Glasgow. They thus established the tradition of the working-class mountaineer, in a sport previously the preserve of the gentleman climber. Andy Sanders, the founder of the Creag Dhu was a Brown's man, and the widening of his horizons and ambitions in the hills had the ultimate result of grooming him for the post of general manager at the yard. And there was Carbeth, of which more later.

There are little bits and pieces of architecture in Clydebank, cameos of pre-1914 styles that are worth a look if you ferret them out. Just east of Brown's yard was the marshalling depot of the

Caledonian Railway Company, and there can be found a couple of the cottages they built for their employees, with the company logo and other sandstone reliefs on the walls. Back on Dumbarton Road is the quaintly named Kizil Mansions, a rather superior tenement in an Art Nouveau style, which survived the Blitz. For it should be remembered that much of Clydebank was destroyed in the Second World War, when only eight houses totally escaped damage.

One third of the 12,000 houses were totally destroyed and the rest damaged to varying degrees, and 500 people were killed in the raids of 1941. And the worst damage was to the working-class tenement areas around the shipyard. North of Brown's, heading back towards the canal, there is little housing left, only a mess of roads, warehouses and a ghastly theme-park-style pool, which was another private but publicly funded venture which went bankrupt and had to be taken over by the local authority. The kind of place where you paddle and eat burgers.

Before we arrive back at Kilbowie Road, there is a huge shopping centre which, with the Business Park, helped the town in the jobs sphere when the worst of the '80s industrial closures were taking place. The canal here sports (so they say) the world's only floating fish-and-chip shop, McMonagles, serving the delicacy from a purpose-built static boat on the canal. As I said before, Clydebank isn't Venice. On Kilbowie Road, you can look up and down its sweep and realise what the Blitz did to the town; elsewhere you would blame the planners, but here they had their work done for them. Back at Singer's, to your right behind some houses is yet another shopping development. This was formerly the ground of Clydebank FC, which they sold to pay debts, but were then unable to find another home. The team now plays in junior football, which is a reflection of the way events have hit the town.

But the Bankies are nothing if not resilient. The population of the burgh has fallen from over 50,000 to under 40,000 in the last 25 years. While the new local jobs are often low paid and unskilled, many of the skilled men in Clydebank refused to give up. The town has the greatest average drive-to-work distance of any in Scotland, and as well as this, many Bankies got jobs in North Sea oil, commuting during the week to Aberdeen, or overseas to areas where their skills were in demand, like the Middle East. What Nazism couldn't kill, Thatcherism didn't either. Even the *Clydebank Press,* founded in 1891, still comes out every week, though now named the *Post.*

At Singer station you can catch a train back to Glasgow. Or you can take the Bankie Trek, which I have written about elsewhere. In the 1930s many folk in Clydebank had huts at a place called Carbeth about ten miles north of the town. These had developed from tents established on a sympathetic landowner's estate pre-WWI, the huts gradually extending to a village of over a hundred. As well as the huts, the Carbeth residents built a swimming pool by damming a burn. And there was a wee shop run by Jimmy Robinson, a fanatical communist, who always had a brew, day or night, for arrivals. This was their weekend and holiday escape, a socialist Butlin's, whose atmosphere is described in Glasser's *Growing up in the Gorbals,* in the chapter 'A Taste of Freedom':

> Talk was of politics, of jobs and apprenticeships, of sex and conquest except when girls were in the party. Those summer nights were not really endless and totally wonderful but they seemed to be. Arrivals in the night were uniquely wonderful, filled with a sense of homecoming to a place where your lungs drew in new air that was your very own. Fellowship of the night. A time for innocents.

Though people like Glasser came from the Gorbals, most of the hutters were from Clydebank. They had no cars so the Bankies walked, up Kilbowie Road, over the Kilpatrick Hills, and then down into Carbeth. (Now you can get a bus from Singers to Faifley, Clydebank's postwar housing estate, and save a couple of miles walking.) During the Blitz when the initial provision for the folk of the town was appalling, many had to spend nights in the open on the Kilpatrick Hills without food or shelter. Those with huts at Carbeth decamped there with their children, and the men walked to the shipyards and factories on Monday morning. You can follow this walk, and find more about the Carbeth experience, at this web address:

www.glasgowwestend.co.uk/people/ianmitch.html

From the Kilpatrick Hills you overlook Clydebank's Auchentoshan Distillery, producer of Scotland's best lowland malt, which advertises itself as 'Glasgow's Whisky'. This proves my point. What a Bankie distillery does, a Buddy one would never do.

I still go back to Clydebank and do the occasional Workers' Educational Association class – or Wrinklies Educational Association as it should be, since those attending are all well over 70. And they are all women, for the men are dead. Some in their 90s lost their men in the war, others' husbands died from asbestosis or from the problems associated with a region where male life-expectancy is generally low. And they have all either been to Carbeth, or knew people in the Creag Dhu, or were members of the Rep or the Lyric, or have a trades union or political background, or any combination of these. And they call me 'son' and they buy my books, though a few of them cannot really afford to, so they get a reduction. And they remind me.

Remind me that some of the best folk who trod this earth were the politicised generation of working-class people who came out of the struggles of the first half of the twentieth century. They were always a minority of their fellows, even in a place like Clydebank. But the Bankie of the species was just that wee cut above the rest.

However nobody is perfect. In the 1970s Clydebank successfully campaigned against incorporation into Glasgow, and for a while had its own council. But they paid the price for this in the 1990s, when another reorganisation put them in West Dunbartonshire. Instead of being a part of the City of Culture where they belong, the Bankies are stuck with Dumbarton and Helensburgh. After the Depression, the Blitz and Thatcherism, they deserve better. So I have annexed them into Glasgow for my book. I can pay them no greater compliment.

Yoker and Scotstoun

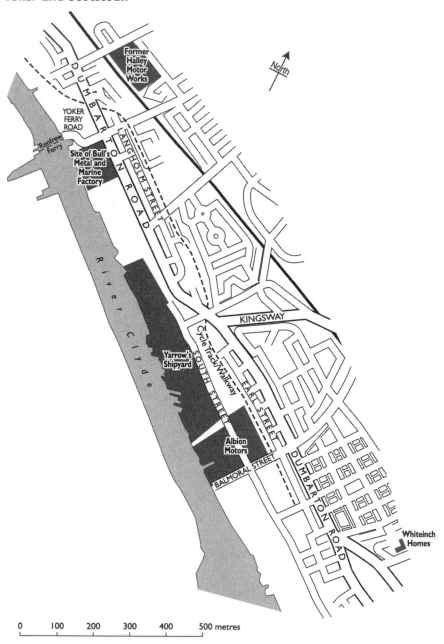

Former Halley Motor Works

YOKER FERRY ROAD

Renfrew Ferry

Site of Bull's Metal and Marine Factory

DUMBARTON ROAD

ANGHOLM STREET

North

River Clyde

Yarrow's Shipyard

SOUTH STREET

Cycle Track/Walkway

KINGSWAY

EARL STREET

Albion Motors

BALMORAL STREET

DUMBARTON ROAD

Whiteinch Homes

0   100   200   300   400   500 metres

CHAPTER SIX

Yokerstoun: Siamese Twins

FOR THE 22 YEARS I worked in Clydebank I went each day through Yoker and Scotstoun. Sometimes by bus along Dumbarton Road, sometimes by one of the two train routes between Glasgow and Clydebank. And many times I cycled, either along the official cycle track by the Clyde, or along the path of the old Forth and Clyde Canal to Clydebank. There is no part of the city whose physical imagery is so fixed in my mind as this composite Yokerstoun. Give me a pen and pencil and from my mental map I could probably produce a pretty accurate street plan and building description of the whole area. In addition, many of my students, both the apprentices and those seeking to gain qualifications for university entry, came from Yokerstoun.

It is a district where pavement pedestrianism might appear to be unpromising. It is not that it is Glasgow's most deprived region; far from it. There are parts of Yoker especially that are grim, but nothing like Dalmarnock or Possil is to be found in the Yokerstoun area. No, it is something else. Both these areas were new ones, which grew up from virtually nothing a century or so ago, and they did not overlay much of previous historical significance. In terms of its built environment, Yokerstoun does not possess many of the qualities that made Glasgow Britain's premier Victorian city. Springburn, for example, is of world historical architectural significance, when compared to Yokerstoun – everything being relative. What makes this area an essential component of any book which deals with working-class Glasgow, is its role in the history of the working-class movement, especially around the time of the First World War. In that perspective primarily, does Yoker – and Scotstoun – gain importance.

Where they meet, like Siamese twins joined at the head, these districts contain two of the historically most important industrial units on Clydeside: Albion Motors in Scotstoun and the adjacent Yarrows shipyard stretching into Yoker. To those who like to brand Glasgow's industry as 'nineteenth-century', it needs to be pointed out that both of these factories date from the twentieth. The Alfred Yarrows ship-yard moved from the Thames to the Clyde in 1906, whilst Albion Motors, mainly a commercial vehicle producer, had opened a couple of years earlier. These were not dinosaurs of the Industrial Revolution, but the highest-tech industries of their day – and for many years to follow. And along with Weirs in Cathcart and the Parkhead Forge, these were the main centres of industrial unrest in the years 1914–19, the key power bases of the Clyde Workers' Committee (CWC). Formerly, these and other industrial units along the Clyde were served by a railway. The closure of this and construction of a cycle track on its bed has provided a convenient vantage point for a traverse of Yokerstoun.

Leaving Whiteinch, the cycle track goes parallel to Earl Street, which lies south of Dumbarton Road. The station platforms where the workers of Albion and Yarrows detrained are still clearly visible at the sides of the cycle track. Now a car park lies to the south of this; and across South Street itself, what remains of Albion Motors. This plant once covered the whole area around the junction of South and Balmoral Streets, now either derelict or warrened with Third World cowboy capitalists. After becoming part of British Leyland in 1951, then DAF motors in the 1980s, then experiencing a management buy out in the '90s, 'the Albion' still survives as Albion Automotive with about 400 workers, making axles and transmission equipment for commercial vehicles. A trip to the Glasgow Transport Museum shows the gorgeous commercial vehicles, buses and lorries, all with the dis-tinctive Albion badge, which used to pour out of these works when they employed many thousands of men.

One of the men they employed was Willie Gallacher, author of *Revolt on the Clyde* (1936). Though starting life as a Paisley Buddy, and later becoming Communist MP for West Fife, Gallacher's political apprenticeship was served in Glasgow. He worked at the Albion on various occasions, until he was sacked after being imprisoned and jailed in 1916 for his part in the fight against conscription. Gallacher became shop stewards' convenor at the Albion and later chairman of the Clyde Workers' Committee. Though he might exaggerate his overall importance in the events of Red Clydeside, there is little doubting Gallacher's role in helping to organise the men at the Albion in support of the Rent Strikes in Glasgow during the war. And he also helped to break the isolation of the Weir's Strike in 1915, turning it into one of national importance. The stewards at Albion called a meeting, and:

> We decided on action with Weir's and called a mass meeting. We also got in touch with Yarrow's and Mechan's to ensure they also took action. The delegation of the Albion, of which I was the leader, arrived at St Mungo Hall ...
>
> I said that I brought greetings from the Albion and a pledge of solidarity as long as the fight lasted. I told them that Yarrow's and Mechan's were on the move. What a scene there was as they jumped to their feet and cheered.

Gallacher added in his book that 'The workers of the Clyde had broken through the rotten atmosphere of war jingoism'. In fact he and his fellow Socialist Labour Party shop stewards avoided criticism of the war in their industrial capacities, and concentrated on economic issues, like wages and the dilution of labour. For this they were criticised by John Maclean, who always put opposition to the war at the forefront on any agitation. But for all his faults there was worse than Willie Gallacher, and after he died in his council flat in 1965 in his native Paisley, 40,000 Buddies followed the coffin or lined the streets. Unrepentant Stalinist as he was, Gallacher was aware of the flaws and weaknesses of his class, but he still loved them and identified with them.

In this Gallacher was unlike another flawed and unrepentant Stalinist who worked here in the Second World War, Hugh MacDiarmid. Gallacher mentions Mechan's in his account of the 1915 strike given above. This was an ironworks which lay beside Albion and Yarrows and was founded about the same time. MacDiarmid, too old to fight, was conscripted into industrial work during World War Two, and the three years he worked at Mechan's formed one of several periods he spent in Glasgow. MacDiarmid is Scotland's greatest twentieth-century poet, possibly the greatest ever, and the only Scot who should have been awarded the Nobel Prize for Literature in my opinion. But he was a horrible, horrible man.

Unlike people such as Gallacher who became socialists because of their sympathy with what they felt capitalism had done to people, MacDiarmid – or Christopher Murray Grieve, as he was born – became a communist through contempt. Glasgow influenced many of his poems, especially his *Hymns to Lenin*, and in these there are lines of majestic outrage. From the *Second Hymn*:

Oh, it's nonsense, nonsense, nonsense,
Nonsense at this time o day
That breid-and-butter problems
S'ud be in ony man's way.
Sport, love, and parentage,
Trade, politics and law,
S'ud be nae mair tae us than braith
We hardly ken we draw.
Freein oor pooers for greater things
And fegs there's plenty o them
Though us that's trammelt in below
Cannae be tenty o them.

At the same time he took refuge in a Nietzschean disdain for ordinary people, seeing the salvation of humanity lying in its imitating his own heroic self. He wrote, appallingly, in *A Drunk Man Looks at the Thistle*, that:

Millions o wimmin bring forth in pain
Millions o bairns that are no worth ha'en.

With his inability to relate to ordinary working men, MacDiarmid's time in Mechan's was torture. He took his breaks and meals alone, and was useless at his work, almost slicing his foot off through carelessness. It is unsurprising that he could not communicate with his fellow workers. In the *Third Hymn to Lenin* he talks of 'Glasgow's hordes' 'all bogged down in words that communicate no thought only mumbo jumbo, fraudulent crap, ballyhoo…'.

Passing further along the cycle track, the Yarrows shipyard is next to the Albion. Still employing 2,500 workers, this must be the largest industrial unit in Glasgow – or even the whole of Clydeside – today. It has largely survived because of the Cold War, since Yarrows was always a warship builder. To the right of the cycle track here lie some curious cottages. Amidst the ubiquitous tenements of Dumbarton Road, these flat-roofed, brick-built buildings are eye-catching. They are known as the Yarrows Cottages, and were built for some of the many English workers who followed the shipyard from the Thames to the Clyde a century ago. I often think the majority of the population of Glasgow about 1900 must have been incomers of one sort or another.

The track then crosses Dumbarton Road, and we have Scotstounhill to the right and Yoker to the left, with something to see each way. On the left the modest sandstone Parish Hall building which commemorated Yoker's brief independence, till it was incorporated by Glasgow in 1926. And on the right on Kingsway are found what must be the best council houses Glasgow ever built, a group of sparkling Art Deco detached blocks, with balconies and steel railings. Naturally these were bought when tenants were allowed to purchase their properties and now change hands for many times the original price. The other council properties in Scotstounhill are not so grand, though it is a well-kept and pleasant area. Not quite the same as Yoker, which takes us to – and beyond – the city boundary.

Dumbarton Road here is pretty run down, and so too is the area around Langholm Street, behind which the cycle track runs before following the former railway route back down towards the River Clyde, passing under Kelso Street. Around here are plenty of dookits, and the ungainfully employed men who tend then, and at the bottom of Kelso Street, the Clyde's last working ferry. Started as a chain-hauled ferry in 1868, the Yoker ferry still runs to Renfrew. Though not carrying cars for the last 20 years or so, it still takes passengers and bikes. The dereliction around hardly encourages use of the ferry, and neither does the payment system.

This I discovered when I decided to take the bike to the green hills of Renfrewshire by the ferry. A machine demanded exact payment of 46p, and I had a 50p coin. Noting the machine took only the exact fare, I asked the crew member not driving the ferry for a ticket.

'We dinnae sell tickets.'

Change?

'We dinnae hae change.'

I went back to Dumbarton Road, made various purchases and eventually found the exact combination of coins for the machine. As we sailed across the Clyde I asked the crew member not driving the ferry, and trying not to sound critical, what his job was.

'It's fur tae collect the tickets when ye get aff. Tae see that ye hiv pyed.'

Both Sides of the Burn was a fine booklet on the history of Yoker produced by the pupils of the now-closed Yoker Secondary. It was 1966 and Yoker was bustling and booming. Half of Yoker is in Clydebank on the west side of the Yoker Burn, the rest being in Glasgow. There was almost nothing at Yoker before the late nineteenth century, apart from Thomas Harvey's distillery, and Colin Robb's Inn which lay on the east side of the burn and was largely used by drovers. The west side of the burn in Clydebank saw the coming of shipbuilding in 1877, but the east side waited till later for industrial development, when some exotic factories came to Yoker. In 1901 John Bull started manufacturing ships' propellors at Bull's Metal and Marine. Despite his very English name, Bull (probably Bulle) was a Norwegian entreprenuer. These works lay just east of the Yoker ferry, and is today part derelict, part covered in housing, and part occupied by a couple of small engineering works.

Another Scandinavian seeking to take advantage of Glasgow's booming economy set up Halley Motors in Yoker, where he manufactured the famous Halley fire engines. Halley was a Dane, and his works were later taken over by Albion Motors. These works are now gone, and so too, probably to the greater relief of Yoker folk, are White's chemical works. These were established beside the Forth and Clyde Canal in north Yoker. We will later come across White, Lord Overtoun, in relation to his chemical works at Shawfield in Rutherglen. The country's leading chrome manufacturer was also for a while its leading iodine manufactuer, and produced this valuable commodity from Highland kelp at Yoker. Though not as polluting as his Rutherglen works, White's Yoker works were no model factory either, as the workers dealt with caustic soda, bleaching soda, and lime in dangerous concentrations. The coming of all these works a century ago filled up the streets between Clydebank and Glasgow with tenements, and streets like Bulldale Street and Halley Street which today commemorate lost employment.

At the end of a working day at Clydebank, if I didn't fancy a two-way cycle, I'd leave the bike at work and take the bus home from college, and this went straight through Yokerstoun, allowing a survey of the Dumbarton Road. At the far end of Yokerstoun, before Dumbarton Road enters Whiteinch, lies a substantial middle-class housing development of villas and terraces, which is now a conservation area. Even in this city with an edge, there are few places where a street provides such a stark social divide as Dumbarton Road does here. When the houses were advertised in 1905 in the *Glasgow Herald*, prospective occupants of properties in Danes Drive, Norse Road and the other streets were reassured that the busy Dumbarton Road divided 'the classes from the masses' at the southern side. And it still does. The most interesting buildings in the whole of Yokerstoun are here, on Westland Drive. Westercraigs was built as an orphanage in 1890, and is a fine sandstone villa still occupied by the Church of Scotland. Next to it is the Whiteinch Homes building, constructed as a poorhouse in 1890 but, very unusually for Scotland, in the style of a medieval English almshouse, round a central courtyard. This building lay vacant for many years, but has been restored as luxury accommodation. From poorhouse to penthouse – albeit ground floor. But not bad for Yokerstoun.

Partick

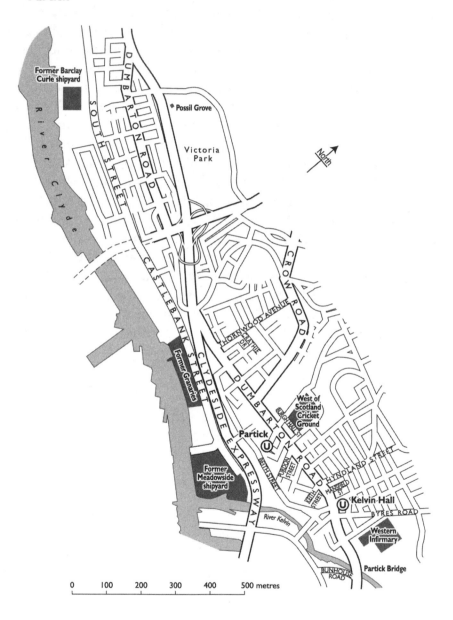

Former Barclay Curle shipyard

Possil Grove

Victoria Park

River Clyde

SOUTH STREET

DUMBARTON ROAD

North

CROW ROAD

CASTLEBANK STREET

HORNWOOD AVENUE

CRATHIE DRIVE

CLYDESIDE EXPRESSWAY

Former Granaries

DUMBARTON ROAD

BENALDER STREET

West of Scotland Cricket Ground

Partick

HYNDLAND STREET

Former Meadowside shipyard

DUNCAN STREET

MANSFIELD ST

KEITH STREET

BEITH STREET

Kelvin Hall

BYRES ROAD

River Kelvin

Western Infirmary

BUNHOUSE ROAD

Partick Bridge

| 0 | 100 | 200 | 300 | 400 | 500 metres |

CHAPTER SEVEN

Partick: Glasgow's Girnal

SUCH HAS BEEN the decline of Scots as the everyday language of Glasgow that not many people would know what a girnal was. The cosmopolitan nature of the city has produced its own argot, which is expressive and creative, but it contains relatively few Scots words. I was surprised on coming here from Aberdeen to find that people didn't know what a brander was, or a scaffie. A century ago, most Glasgow folk would still have known that a girnal was a grain chest and that Partick was the area where was landed and processed most of the city's grain.

Partick's eastern border with the city was the River Kelvin, which falls steeply to the Clyde, and which powered the early granaries along its banks. And here today survives the city's last grain mill. This is owned by Rank Hovis and produces flour for their Duke Street bakery. Timothy Pont's map of Lennox c 1600 shows a cluster of mills on the lower river, including Bishop's Mill and a meal mill leased by the city of Glasgow. The incorporation of Glasgow bakers also owned two mills on the river, one called the Bunhouse Mill. Although other works, such as spinning and (timber) slit mills used the water power of the Kelvin, it was grain mills which predominated.

Large-scale industrial flour milling began with the opening of the Scotstoun Mills in the 1840s, though as the Kelvin provided such cheap and efficient power, these were still water-operated, and remained so till the later expansion in the nineteenth century, when steam was applied. The Regent Flour mills were built across the Kelvin from the Scotstoun mill in the 1890s. Owned by the SCWS from 1903, this mill made the famous Lofty Peak flour (the site is now a car park for the Kelvin Hall). This cluster of mills large and small made it logical for the Clyde Navigation Trust to establish its grain depot at Meadowside in Partick in the early 1900s, and until very recently the origin of most material for Glasgow's ubiquitous *jeely peece* was in the girnals of Partick.

A good place to start an exploration of the area is at the bridge over the Kelvin, built to join Partick with Glasgow in 1877, just west of the Kelvin Hall. One end of the bridge bears the Glasgow coat of arms, the other that of Partick – which appropriately has millstones and a wheatsheaf on its crest. These crests are found on the cast-iron supports of the bridge. The previous bridge lies just to the north and is still open to pedestrians. From here a walk down Bunhouse Road, and right along Old Dumbarton Road brings you to the Wheatsheaf Buildings. Now flats, this cameo was built in the 1830s on the site of the original Bishop's Mill, and has delightful wheatsheaf motifs carved on its gables. It operated as a mill till the 1960s, and was water-driven till the 1950s.

No such new use has been found for the derelict Partick Central station further on, though the land released by demolishing part of the Scotstoun Flour mills is now occcupied by stunning modern flats. Partick is being squeezed between the West End and the Riverside, old and new middle-class residential areas. A huge cleared site to the west of Partick Central awaits residential development, as a corridor to connect the riverside to the West End. This was formerly the Partick Foundry and after closure in the '60s became the site of unsightly scrap metal depots. However, back around 1600 this was the site chosen for the building of Partick Castle, a fortified house serving as the country home of George Hutcheson, co-founder of Glasgow Hutcheson's Hospital. Partick Castle was demolished in 1836.

Given its location (West End, University, Kelvingrove Museum etc) and facilities (subway, railway, expressway) Partick has become a classic example of the benefits – or drawbacks depending on your view – of the process of gentrification. It can't be long before the owners of the last operating grain mill realise that they can make a lot more money selling the land for housing than using it to employ millers and make flour. Gentrification promotes de-industrialisation, as well as resulting from it.

Before heading along Beith Street it is worth visiting Glasgow's smallest graveyard. In amongst some modern housing on Keith Street lies the Quaker burial ground. Surrounded with metal railings, it has no gravestones, but a wooden plaque stating its function:

SOCIETY of FRIENDS
BURIAL GROUND
Gifted by
JOHN PURDON 1711
LAST USED 11-XII-1857

The Quakers gifted the land to Partick, and a part of it was used for road building – in return for the site being kept in good order (which it appears to be) – and for 1s a year being donated to the Society of Friends. Does the Kooncil still pay the 5p? Apparently Purdon's wife was the first interred in the cemetery, and the family, which was a prominent one in eighteenth-century Partick, is commemorated in neighbouring Purdon Street.

This area is the heart of the old pre-industrial village of Partick, and Keith Street used to be known as the Goat. The 'goat' in question was not four-footed, but an old Scots name for a small burn, one of which ran here. At the north end of the Goat was the Heid o' the Goat, a place where acrobats, quack doctors and religious and political agitators held court. A nineteenth-century Partick poet, Tom Burns, describes the scene:

> Though its richt name's in print on a prominent spot
> The ane its best kent by is the heid o the Goat
> There tradesmen o every class you will find
> In guid Doric language expressing their mind

The old cottage buildings here were only demolished in the 1930s, and the Heid o' the Goat is now the Comet carpark.

Along Beith Street are renovated sandstone tenements and some fine new flats, but the most interesting building is the former Partick Fire Station, dating from 1906. This too has been converted to housing though the brick fire tower has been retained as a feature. The building itself is mostly brick-built, unusual for Glasgow before 1914, and also done in an almost Germanic style of architecture: Potsdam rather than Partick. Just beside the fire station at Meadow Road access is gained to the Clydeside cycletrack, which provides a high and traffic-free vantage point for further sightseeing.

The whole skyline to the south is dominated by cranes. But not shipyard cranes as would once have been the case, but building cranes, for the riverside here is the site of a multi-million pound redevelopment, dominated by new housing. Partick was never the shipbuilding centre that Govan was, but it did have some important yards. From the cycletrack, looking back towards the Kelvin's mouth, can still be seen the derelict brick and sandstone offices of the Meadowside Shipbuilding Yard, with its central tower in a sort of French Renaissance style. Hopefully this will survive redevelopment in some form. One of the early owners of this yard, David Tod, became the first provost of Partick. The second provost was John White, owner of the Scotstoun Mills, showing the tendency in the nineteenth century for local capitalists to exercise almost feudal (that is, uniting the political and the economic) powers in their locales, as provosts, MPs, JPs and the like.

Across the Kelvin mouth lay Inglis's Pointhouse yard, which specialised in paddle steamers, building the current *Waverley* in 1947, and the one of the same name which it replaced, which was sunk at Dunkirk in 1940. The *Maid of the Loch*, currently being refurbished as an attraction at the Loch Lomond National Park, was built by Inglis's in 1952, but the yard closed ten years later, ending shipbuilding on the Kelvin.

Between Meadowside and Whiteinch to the west, the Partick riverside was dominated by granaries. Inglis's yard had a famous set of sheer legs, 96 feet high that stood till 1965, but they were puny beside the 13-storey brick granary built by the Clyde Navigation Trust in 1911–13, at a cost of £130,000 (which would not pay for half of one of the flats being constructed on its ruins). Partick Thistle's move to Maryhill in 1909, after over 30 years in Partick, was occasioned by the purchase of their stadium for construction of the granaries. In 1937 another granary, equally large, was built adjacent to the original one, and this Meadowside girnal of Glasgow could claim for a while to be one of the world's largest brick buildings. It gave a curiously reassuring feeling to see its bulk, and many people united in opposition to its destruction, arguing that the granary itself could have been converted to housing. Though the developers successfully argued against this, a significant part of the original construction materials were recycled into the new buildings.

Whether these new residents will consider themselves Partickonians remains to be seen. The construction of the Clydeside expressway separated Partick from the River Clyde, and it also cut Partick itself asunder. At the Thornwood Roundabout, Dumbarton Road disappears under the Expressway, in a maze of flyovers, to re-emerge in the rather forlorn district of Whiteinch. Few people consider it so today, but from its foundation Whiteinch was part of Partick burgh. Very little was found hereabouts till the Barclay Curle shipyard opened in the 1870s, moving from Anderston. Starting with clippers and ending with liners, and building almost everything else in between, Barclay Curle was one of Glasgow's finest shipyards, a specialist builder which even managed to operate fully during the 1930s Depression. The yard has been demolished but the marine engine works Barclay Curle built just before World War One remain, with their fine hammerhead crane and the (listed) mansard roof enlivening the skyline.

Whiteinch at one time was almost a model village. South of Dumbarton Road were the tenements for the workers in the shipyard, and to the north were rows of modest villas, Gordon Park, built in the 1880s for workers from the Scotstoun estate. These, clustered round the bowling green, now form a conservation area. Cut off from Partick by the expressway, Whiteinch was also cut off from Victoria Park to the north by the same road, which took over a slice of the park itself. A stroll through the park will not only bring you back to Partick proper, but also allow you to see the world-famous Fossil Grove which it contains. Not just one, but a whole stand of fossilised scale trees, over 250 million years old, with their trunk-like roots, excellently preserved. Again, though not generally thought of as Partick today, Victoria Park was actually laid out by the burgh.

Renegotiating the over- and underpasses of the expressway brings you to the bottom of Thornwood Drive, cursing the negative effects such roads have on urban communities – and on urban pedestrianism. Thornwood has always had the reputation of being the posh part of Partick. Fine red sandstone tenements, well maintained and inhabited by the prosperous and respectable working and lower-middle classes. There can be a monotony in respectability but in Thornwood this is broken by some of the best council housing in the city. There are blocks of good municipal housing, and at Crathie Drive is a building of exceptional merit and interest which dominates the Thornwood skyline. This is Crathie Court, built in 1952, but its

Art Deco features show pre-war design influence in the projecting balconies and lines of porthole windows. Set in well-maintained grounds, the building was designed as 88 flats for single people at a time when almost all housing was for the standard nuclear family. In recognition of its importance the building gained a Saltire Award. Crow Road takes us back down to Dumbarton Road, and slightly more scruffy East Partick.

But even here the relentless march of gentrification continues. Up Norval Street, off Crow Road, generations of Pertick wummen toiled in Tomlinson's factory making cardboard boxes; you could watch them from the passing blue trains at Partick Station. Today its bright pastel exterior and atrium roof proclaim it as The Printworks apartment block.

Moving along Dumbarton Road is a pleasant pedestrian experience, as the line of the street is virtually unbroken and the commercial premises are all occupied and well maintained, in contrast to those in Whiteinch. It was not always so pleasant however, and in 1875 a procession of Irish nationalists on Dumbarton Road was attacked by political opponents, leading to three days of rioting. This was ended only when special constables were sworn in, to support the police in quelling the disturbances. Partick's other great unrest was in the Rent Strikes of 1915 when the area was one of the strongest in the city for action against profiteering. These struggles were led by the Partick housewives, harrassing the landlords' agents with hails of refuse and laying about them with pots and pans. The women in turn were led by ILP member, Helen Crawfurd. The women of Partick appear a fierce brood. A famous nineteenth-century Partick lass was Big Rachael, all 6 foot 4 inches and 16 stones of her. She worked as a labourer in the Meadowside yard and later as a foreman (-person?) in a brickworks. In the riots of 1875 she was enrolled as a special constable.

Before 1914 Partick was a stronghold of Orangeism, especially its shipyards where many had come to work from Ulster; it is not generally recognised that 40% of the city's Irish immigration came from Ulster – this was largely responsible for bringing the poison of sectarianism to Glasgow. John Paton, in his *Proletarian Pilgrimage*, writes of his dismay at finding such a phenomenon in Glasgow, so absent in his native Aberdeen. Paton's book was published in the 1930s, and describes how before World War One an ILP propaganda lorry was set ablaze by Orangemen in Partick, and the comrades decided to assert their right of free speech by a march along Dumbarton Road. They were ambushed by well-organised groups emerging from closes to attack the procession. Paton comments:

> We'd no chance at all against them. They were tough fellows from the shipyards who enjoyed nothing so much as a good fight. It wasn't a defeat, it was a rout.

However, even before the war these diehard Tory Orangemen were prepared to listen to socialist speakers, rather than simply attack them. Paton recounts the factory gate meeting at a Whiteinch shipyard (probably Barclay Curle's), addressed by his fellow Aberdonian, Jamie Kessack. Immediately grasping their attention by his opening words:

> Last Sunday I stood on the Custom House steps at Belfast, girdled by the steel of the bayonets of the circle of soldiers who enclosed me ...

Kessack got a 'rapt audience and hearty applause at the end'. The war and its aftermath seriously weakened, though did not kill, political Orangeism.

A wee trip off Dumbarton Road to Burgh Hall Street allows us to take a look at the centre of Partick government from 1852 till 1912. In that latter year an Act of Parliament overturned Partick's wishes to remain independent, and a piper played *Lochaber no more*. Would that, a century on, our politicians had the courage to similarly add Glasgow's present periphery to the city. But Partick, Govan and Maryhill were working-class areas; Bearsden and Newton Mearns are not.

Partick Burgh Halls, though well used and under renovation, cannot compete with those of Maryhill and Govan, either in exterior embellishment or interior furnishings. But it certainly has a better view, looking out as it does across the lawns of the West of Scotland Cricket ground to the villas of Partickhill rising beyond. Once a curling pond and bowling green, the site has a place in football history, in that it hosted the first Scotland–England international in 1872. Not only roads and railways can separate social classes, so too can parks, or sports fields, and while at the north end of the cricket ground you are in patrician Partickhill, on the south you are in proletarian Partick. Partick Library, which is passed on the right heading back to the Cross, used to have a nice wee exhibition on the history of the area, though it was missing on my last visit.

Between Hyndland Street and Mansfield Street is one of the few cleared areas on Dumbarton Road, where a block of tenements was demolished to make way for a recreation area. This could be better maintained, and the Friends of Mansfield Park are working hard at it. On Mansfield Street is found the offices of *An Commun Ghaidhlig* (dedicated to promoting Gaelic and language) and a Gaelic bookshop, occupying the ground floor of a solid set of tenements, built, as it proudly states, by the St George's Co-operative Society. It is appropriate that this is located here as Partick has always had a tradition of Gaelic immigrants and Gaelic churches. It is estimated that in Partick and the wider West End of Glasgow there is a greater concentration of Gaelic speakers than anywhere outside Lewis in the Western Isles.

Though this tradition was swelled by the influx of Gaels to work on various jobs on the Clyde, it goes further back to when Partick was on the drove route into Glasgow from the West Highlands. The drovers came down what is now Crow Road (Crow is from the Gaelic *croadh*, cattle) and overnighted in Partick before moving into Glasgow. A famous inn, Granny Gibbs's, was the destination of these drovers, and lay near the present Thornwood roundabout. This inn was built by Granny Gibbs's husband in 1796 when droving was at its height, and demolished a century later, when it had ended. Drovers kept their sheep and cattle in her pens, before moving into Glasgow. Her thatched dwelling was commemorated by another of the prolific Partick poets, George Boyce:

The drovers passing east and west
Knew her wee hoose of call
With Highland whisky o the best
She would supply them all.

This tradition of Highland hostelry continues in the pub on the corner of Mansfield Street, the Lismore, which does much to support Gaelic music and culture. The owners have also commissioned a set of fine stained-glass windows in the pub, commemorating the Highland Clearances, and showing Highlanders at work. These panels have clearly been influenced by those of Stephen Adam in Maryhill Burgh Halls (see Unlocking Maryhill). Partick's taverns have a long tradition of conviviality. Bunhouse Road is not named after a bakery but after an inn called the Bun and Yill Hoose which formerly stood there. In Strang's *Glasgow and its Clubs* we read of the Partick Duck Club, which flourished in the early nineteenth century. This group of Glasgow worthies were mainly from the Trades House, and used to repair to Partick to feast at the Bun Hoose on roast duck and peas, washed down with punch. One of their number was immortalised in the couplet:

The ducks of Partick quacked for fear
Crying 'Lord preserve us, there's MacTear!'

The profusion of fat ducks in Partick was due to their feasting on the products and by-products of the grain mills on the Kelvin. The old Bun Hoose apparently had a lintel dated 1695 over the door, but was demolished in 1849.

Back at the foot of Byres Road we are at Partick Cross. Here is a curious scene. On the one hand good-quality red sandstone tenements, and on the other every inch of vacant land being filled with lofts and appartments. On the one hand the spread of upmarket restaurants and cafés, on the other the survival of little works, almost sweatshops – and probably the greatest concentration of charity shops in Glasgow. Does this signify a hidden poverty in Partick, or just that the nearby denizens of the more prosperous West End areas can spot a bargain when they see one? Its worst housing long ago demolished by the expressway, Partick does not give out the air of dereliction of some other inner-city working-class areas of Glasgow. Its population, which grew from about 5,000 in 1852 to 56,000 in 1912, has declined to about 40,000 today, but is rising again.

The university was never in Partick. But the Western Infirmary, or rather the Anderson College of Medicine as it originally was, did lie within the burgh boundaries – but only just – after the institution was moved from Glasgow in 1889. A dramatic relief by Pittendrigh MacGillivray adorns the building, showing doctors performing an operation. He was an Aberdeen artist who did much work in Glasgow, and whose sculptures of shipyard workers in Govan we have already noted. Just within Partick also, and bearing an address in Dumbarton Road, is the curious Tudor Cottage on the north bank of the Kelvin, within Kelvingrove Park. This was an exhibit of model workers' housing from Leverhume's Port Sunlight factory on Merseyside. It was shown at the International Exhibition in Kelvingrove in 1901, and later donated to the city for use as a park-keeper's dwelling. This is the last, or first, dwelling in Partick and a good place to end.

In 1912 they played *Lochaber no more*; such is the rate of change in Partick, as it becomes swallowed up by the West End of Glasgow, that it may soon be *Partick no more*. Close to the West End, close to the university, close to the Art Gallery, Partick was always that bit different from other working-class areas in Glasgow.

Anderston

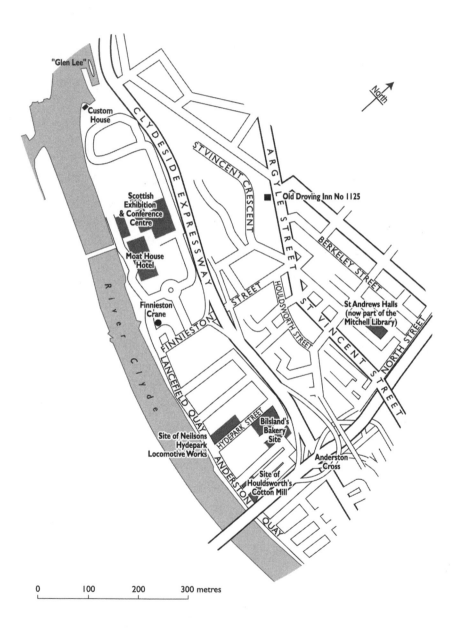

"Glen Lee"

Custom House

CLYDESIDE EXPRESSWAY

ST VINCENT CRESCENT

ARGYLE STREET

North

Old Droving Inn No 1125

Scottish Exhibition & Conference Centre

BERKELEY STREET

Moat House Hotel

ST VINCENT STREET

HOULDSWORTH STREET

St Andrews Halls (now part of the Mitchell Library)

Finnieston Crane

River Clyde

NORTH STREET

FINNIESTON STREET

LANCEFIELD QUAY

HYDEPARK STREET

Site of Neilsons Hydepark Locomotive Works

Bilsland's Bakery Site

ANDERSTON

Anderston Cross

Site of Houldsworth's Cotton Mill

ANDERSTON QUAY

| 0 | 100 | 200 | 300 metres |

78

CHAPTER EIGHT

Anderston: Glasgow's Barometer

'GLASGOW MADE THE CLYDE and the Clyde made Glasgow', so the old saying goes.

From my window in Saint Vincent Crescent on the edge of the Anderston district, I watched for over two decades as Glasgow has remade its river in the hope that the new Clyde will help remake Glasgow. Initially I looked out to a Clyde past its industrial greatness, but still alive. From the giant crane at Finnieston, boilers and desalination plants would be lifted onto ships to be exported over the globe. The trio of smaller cranes at the iron ore terminal across the Clyde still unloaded cargoes of iron ore for Ravenscraig and other steelworks. At New Year there were enough ships docked on the river to play a symphony on their sirens to announce midnight. Now, there is only the *Waverley* paddle-steamer.

A nightmare period ensued, as the cranes were blown up and the docks were filled in. The warehouses were demolished, and splendid industrial architecture, such as the Italianate Custom House, fell into decay. The Garden Festival in 1988 briefly gave a facelift to the riverside, but just as swiftly the cosmetic effect faded with little permanent left behind. Today it is different. While not everyone might approve of all that is happening on the banks of the Clyde, such as the new futuristic edifices appearing like mushrooms, there is more activity on the river, and more optimism for the future, than for decades. I am a frequent walker by the river and it is easy – but possibly misplaced – to be nostaglic about its great industrial and seafaring past. On one walk I met an 80-year-old man from Kinning Park, who similarly walks the banks. He told me he had been a docker on the river all his life; when his docker father had lost his job in the 1930s, Wee (he was tiny) Matt admitted he stayed alive by stealing the cream off what he delivered as a milk boy. 'It's much better noo,' Matt was definite, 'The weans hae thae computers and things. They widnae want ma life.'

St Vincent Crescent Lane leads to Kelvinhaugh Street, and a short distance away behind Yorkhill Hospital lies Kelvinhaugh Primary School, built in Victoria's Jubilee in 1887, with a sculpture of Old Vic frowning down at you from the walls. Its original pupils looked down from their heights to the docks of the Second City of the Empire, which had been opened by Victoria herself in 1877, on the site of the demolished Stobcross Mansion House. Now those children's successors look up from their play over a futuristic landscape, but one which still retains images of the past in the former Custom House and the masts of the *Glenlee*, a nineteenth-century cargo sailing ship, 'Glasgow's ship'. The Custom House was restored as a restaurant, failed, and is now the *Glenlee* exhibition centre. This site awaits the arrival of the new Transport Museum, and can be reached from Kelvinhaugh Street by a footbridge over the Clydeside Expressway.

A good point from which to view the changing river is the walkway which passes the Moat House Hotel. No tradition here, but stark modernity in the phallic black-glass hotel and the SECC, Glasgow's copy of the Sydney Opera House (Glasgow is brash enough to copy anything; across the river is the Grand Old Opry, an answer to Memphis's). The site of the SECC saw Glasgow's biggest demonstration since the days of the UCS work-in in the early 1970s. In the spring of 2003, as he prepared to take us into the disaster of the Iraq war, Blair was due to address the Labour Party Conference at the SECC. Eighty thousand people turned up at the SECC in the afternoon to protest against the war, showing that Glasgow may have lost most of its industry, but it has not lost its radical traditions. Blair, however, sneaked in in the morning, did his speech, and made himself scarce.

Also across the river is the new Science Centre, looking like a dinosaur nesting-site from *Jurassic Park*, and there too will be the future BBC headquarters once a new access bridge is built. But again relics of the past mingle pleasingly with the present, in the black lattice-work of the Finnieston Crane, installed in 1935. Last used in the early 1980s, 'the cran' is now a symbol of Glasgow (though, ironically, it was built by Cowans and Sheldon in Carlisle). The main function of the Finnieston Crane was to lift the locomotives, driven down the tramlines from Springburn, onto the waiting transport ships. Beneath the cran is the City Inn, a rather functional-looking new hotel, but whose splendid food belies its image, and where a riverside terrace, the only one in Glasgow, allows a refreshment stop. The south side of the river is now being repopulated, with imaginative pyramidal blocks of flats, next to ones of more conventional design, but painted a riot of pastel colours in an attempt to brighten up the grey Glasgow light. This has not met with universal approval, but I like it.

Both banks of the river here are being lined with new expensive apartment dwellings, many of innovative and striking design, or with former warehouses, coverted to flats. Amongst all this is a fond relic of the past, the *Waverley,* and if it is in port, the world's last ocean-going paddle steamer, built in Glasgow in 1947, is a photo opportunity not to be missed. Its berth has been moved to the Science Centre from its former Kingston Bridge location. The bridge towered over the brick-and-tile palace of Snodgrass's Washington Grain Mills, a building which reminded us that this was granary country. It was a construction that seemed as if it should have been in the middle of the American Prairies or Chicago. Still miraculously in operation as a grain mill in the late 1990s, it was acquired for reconstruction but regrettably has been demolished to provide land for new build.

Also due for demolition is the empty former lodging house beside the Kingston Bridge. Anderston was always the centre of Glasgow's 'models', having five out of the city's 19 such institutions before WWI, even though Anderston had a mere 5% of the city's population. Most of the people who used to work on the riverside hereabouts lived in the district of Anderston. From a single habitation in the middle of the eighteenth century, Anderston had achieved a population of over 30,000 to become one of the most crowded districts in Glasgow by 1900.

Originally called Stobcross, Anderston was planned as a weavers' village in the 1720s by one Anderson, owner of the Stobcross estate. A Weavers Society was formed in 1738. Anderston prospered and grew to a population of 4,000 in the 1790s when weaving fortunes were at their height. The women worked in the spinning industry and the first spinning mill was established about 1750 by Henry Menteith, who brought over 50 French female workers to teach the locals. Henry had fought against the Jacobites at Falkirk in 1746, and had previously had his cattle stolen for refusing to pay blackmail to Rob Roy (of whom more later).

Thomas Sulman's 'Glasgow' *Illustrated London News* (1861)
Anderston from the air

Showing the purely industrial areas of the Clyde, through the mixed industrial and working
class housing areas, to the middle-class developments around the Kelvingrove Park.

Glasgow City Council (Museums)

About 1800 Henry Houldsworth opened one of the first steam-powered cotton spinning factories in Scotland at Cheapside Street in Anderston. This was built without a piece of wood in it, to be fire-proof. Houldsworth became Anderston's first Provost when it became a burgh in 1824, only for it to be annexed by Glasgow in 1846. Hard times in the 1830s caused Houldsworth and other employers to cut wages and the Association of Operative Cotton Spinners called a strike. One nab (or scab) was shot and killed, and in a show-trial five of the leaders of the union were charged with mur-der, acquitted but convicted of a lesser charge and sentenced to transportation, later commuted to various terms of inprisonment. Meanwhile the witnesses shared a £500 reward and emigrated. The strike and the repression crippled the union. On a lighter note this period of textile dominance produced the famous song *The Bleacher Lass o' Kelvinhaugh*, whose heroine worked in the Anderston mills:

Says I 'My lassie where are you going?
What do you do by the Broomielaw?'
Says she, 'Kind sir I'm a bleacher lassie
In Cochrane's Bleachfields in Kelvinhaugh.'

As elsewhere in Glasgow, textiles gave way to heavy engineering, and just as it can claim to be the birthplace of Glasgow's textile indus-try, so Anderston can claim to be the birthplace of many of its heavy industries. The first shipyard on the Upper Clyde was the Stobcross yard of Barclay and Curle, opened in 1818 before moving in 1870 to Whiteinch. William Simpson ('Crimea' Simpson, so-called because he was the official war artist in that conflict) was born in Anderston and painted an interesting picture of a launch at this yard, published in his *Glasgow in the Forties*. Nielson's locomotive works were set up in Hydepark Street, to be near the river, but moved to Springburn (though retaining the Hydepark Works name) in 1876. Similarly William Macfarlane's Saracen Foundry moved to Anderston in the 1860s from the East End, but then moved to a green-field site in Possil. The problem for all these large-scale enterprises was lack of space to expand in the crowded riverside district, and as they grew they moved out. Thus Anderston was again a pointer towards Glasgow's industrial future, in that well before 1914 the area was moving towards dependence on the service and unskilled industries, towards de-skilling and de-industrialisation.

By 1914 the area's employment was dominated by casual and unskilled labour for men in the docks and warehouses, and by industrial employment such as textiles and bakeries which had a largely unskilled female labour force. Bilsland's Bakery was opened here in the 1880s by William Bilsland, who soon afterwards became Provost of Glasgow. Its red-brick construction, with the firm's name visible, still dominates the skyline view to the river, but the bakery is long closed and the building is now honeycombed by small industrial and commercial units. As it became impoverished, Anderston became increasingly overcrowded as people sought to pay lower rents. Much of the housing in Anderston was not of the best quality anyway, and looking at old photographs of its grim and blackened streets provokes little nostalgia. In 1907 the *Glasgow Herald* characterised Anderston as a district where men could be found, 'loitering in a stagnant pool about certain large centres of employment and doing an odd day's work now and again.' Though some of the worst housing was demolished in the 1930s, by 1951 Anderston still had 50% of its people living without an inside toilet and a population density of 1.5 to a room – and in the bad bits it was worse.

This is not to say Anderston was all slum: there was a better part which lay to the north of St Vincent Street, toward the Mitchell Library and the St Andrews Halls. Here lived many who worked in the Wylie and Lochead Cabinetmakers' works, good steady well paid work. This works has now been converted into the block of flats south of the Mitchell Library. 'The Mitchell' is well known as Europe's largest public reference library, but the St Andrew's Hall was destroyed by a fire in the 1960s and rebuilt as a Mitchell extension. The Halls were the scene of many political meetings, most especially the rowdy confrontation between the Clyde Workers' Committee and Lloyd George in 1915 over the dilution crisis. The shop stewards of the engineering works wanted wage rises and workers' control over the dilution of labour, and had organised strikes to press their aims. John Maclean argued that these demands were tantamount to workers' control over the war effort, which the CWC should instead have been opposing.

Anderston's reputation as one of Glasgow's poorest areas with terrible housing meant that when Comprehensive Redevelopment became the vogue in the 1960s, little of the area was destined to remain standing. But much more was demolished than was necessary, the reason being quite simply that land was needed for the M8 motorway and the Kingston Bridge. When this opened in 1970 much of Anderston simply vanished, including entire streets such as Stobcross Street. Anderston admittedly had not a vast amount worth saving, but the demolition of Anderston Cross, with JJ Burnet's marvellous railway station building, built in 1896, was an atrocity. Anderston in fact lost two Crosses to redevelopment. Peden's Cross used to be at the corner of Argyll Street and Elderslie Steet, and was named after a building with a representation of the Covenanter prophet sculpted on it. Alexander Peden reputedly stood here sometime in the mid-seventeenth century and prophesied that the site would become the centre, or the new Cross, of Glasgow. To some extent with the M8 nearby, it has become so.

These developments reduced the population of Anderston to about 10,000 by 1981, which was just about what it was when annexed by Glasgow in 1846. In the last two decades, like some other inner-city working-class areas, the population has been rising again as new housing is constructed on brown sites or as former factories and warehouses are converted to flats. Pleasing 1990s Housing Association blocks in pastel shades with balconies have been built on Argyll Street, one with a doorway commemorating the Anderston Weavers Society. These are mingled with the severer '60s architecture of Anderston, and the look of the area is softening. The 'Anderston Wall' in Argyll Street might seem to be an example of the worst of 60s architecture, but look closely and you will see not a broken window, no graffiti – and no litter. And that is true of Anderston in general; it is, for some reason, the least litter-strewn and grafitti-ridden inner-city area of Glasgow.

At a detached bit of Argyll Street is a wonderful tenement building in Art Nouveau style, the Glasgow Savings Bank, with ornate metal work, fine sandstone sculptures and a marvellous coloured mosaic over the entrance doorway. Built by James Salmon II around 1900, this has suffered some neglect and unwelcome additions, but still must be one of Glasgow's finest tenements. Another tenement block nearer town houses the Buttery, a famous Glasgow restaurant, in what was possibly, from the evidence of the symbols on it, housing built by the Freemasons Society. These two are the only tenements left in the heart of what was formerly Anderston's tenement core.

Further along Houldsworth Street, past the pyramidal Anderston Church, an unsuccessful '60s attempt at modernity, and past the Salvation Army headquarters, lie some semi-derelict nineteenth-century warehouses and factory buildings. These have ornate brickwork and windows, and are well worth restoring, and they give you an impression of what this area was like until 1950: a dense warren of factories and tenements, now to be seen only in old photographs. Anderston's poverty was reflected in the fact that the first Salvation Army foundation in Scotland was opened here in 1879, a presence which continues today. Another first was the Lipton's store in Stobcross Street in 1871, which began the grocer's empire.

It may seem strange that the heavily industrial area of Anderston, which was one of the poorest in Glasgow, lay cheek by jowl with one of the city's more prestigious middle-class developments. But from these derelict factory properties in Houldsworth Street can be seen the impressive wrought-iron ornamentation of a former Edwardian public toilet at the entrance to Minerva Street, which in turn leads to St Vincent Crescent. It was originally called Stobcross Crescent, but the residents thought St Vincent sounded more upmarket, and changed the name.

As Glasgow developed in the nineteenth century, and the centre and east became crowded and polluted, the middle classes moved west. On the Stobcross estate an extensive development of terraced flats was planned, with pleasure gardens, curling ponds and the like, subsequent to Anderston's incorporation into Glasgow in the 1840s. Minerva Street was built in 1849 in a rather Edinburgh style – with its top-curved ground-floor windows – and then work on the Crescent began, being finally finished in 1851. The architect was Alexander Kirkland, who himself lived in a flat in the Crescent. There was a problem of avoiding monotony in the longest crescent in Britain outside Royal Crescent in Bath. Kirkland did this through its serpentine form, by having pillared porticos at irregular intervals

Panel 1. Weavers Struggles … The Calton Weavers Massacre,
People's Palace History Paintings, Ken Currie, 1987
A dispute that was the first real labour conflict in Scottish history.
Six weavers were killed by soldiers.

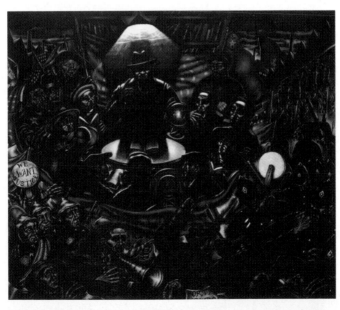

Panel 5. Red Clyde 'We Can Make Glasgow A Petrogad, A Revolutionary Storm
Centre Second To None', People's Palace History Paintings, Ken Currie, 1987
Illustrates John Maclean in typical admonishing, pedagogic pose, with scenes
from the Red Clydeside years depicted around him.
Note how neat and tidy he was.

Cotton Spinners' T. V. Tin Tray, anon. circa 1830s. A fine example of working class domestic culture, showing a mixture of class consciousness and nationalism in its mottoes.

Glasgow City Council (Museums)

Templeton's Carpet Factory, anon., circa 1900
Glasgow's factories were often the first, or the biggest in their particular industry. Sometimes they were also the most beautiful, as with Leiper's design here for the carpet factory facing the Green.

Glasgow City Council (Museums)

John Maclean's memorial, Pollokshaws
John Maclean's memorial, with the tower of the old Burgh Halls behind. One of Maclean's favourite meeting places.
Ian R Mitchell

Female Munitions Worker, William Meikle, War Memorial panel from North British Locomotive Works, 1921
Adam's pupil Meikle produced this over 40 years after the other stained glass works. It shows a female munitions worker at her machine – but incorrectly shows the lathe as left handed.
Ian R Mitchell

The Chemical Worker, Stephen Adam, Maryhill Burgh Halls, 1878
This industry was huge in Victorian Glasgow, with Tennant's St Rollox works the largest in the
world. There were many smaller chemical works, as shown.

The Glassblower, Stephen Adam, Maryhill Burgh Halls, 1878
Maryhill was the centre of Glasgow's rolled and blown glass industries, located on
Murano Street, named after the Venice Glassworks.

The Bricklayers, Stephen Adam, Maryhill Burgh Halls, 1878
Glasgow pre-1914 was built of stone, though there were some brick buildings put up.
Bricklayers had lower status, and wages, than stonemasons.

The Iron Moulders, Stephen Adam, Maryhill Burgh Halls, 1878
Iron moulding was a big employer before World War One. Though the centre of the trade
was in Possil, Maryhill had several smaller ironworks.

The Gas Worker, Stephen Adam, Maryhill Burgh Halls, 1878
Gasworkers were some of the first to form unskilled unions, and were involved in the New Unionism of the 1880s just a few years after this panel was created.

The Railwaymen, Stephen Adam, Maryhill Burgh Halls, 1878
Another of the first to form trade unions, the railwaymen were involved in the strike of 1891. These men are shown at Maryhill Station.

The Calico Workers, Stephen Adam, Maryhill Burgh Halls, 1878
Calico printing was at its height in the first half of the nineteenth century, and in decline by the time Adam made this charming study of women at work.

The Bargee, Stephen Adam, Maryhill Burgh Halls, 1878
The most pastoral of Adam's stained glass panels shows a bargeman with his Clydesdale horse at work along the Maryhill canals.

Muslin Street, Bridgeton, John Quinton Pringle
Pringle's painting of Bridgeton in c1890 shows that, although industry has arrived, the
tenements are still some way from dominating the housing scene.

City Arts Centre, Edinburgh

The Loom, John Quinton Pringle
Although mass domestic weaving died out by about 1850, a few doggedly continued to ply
their trade for some years afterwards, as here shown.

City Arts Centre, Edinburgh

Barclay and Curle's slipdock 1845, William Simpson, 1898
The shipyard in Anderston before it moved to Whiteinch, and when it was still building
wooden sailing ships, as well as steam-driven iron ones.

Glasgow City Council (Museums)

Barclay and Curle's, 2005
The B-listed mansard-roofed engine shop (with crane) of Barclay, Curle and Co. in Whiteinch.

Ian R Mitchell

Hamiltonhill Allotments
The former allotments in Hamiltonhill, showing a bilingual welcome sign. The allotments have since been closed due to concerns over contamination of the soil from previous industrial activity, but may soon be reopened.
Ian R Mitchell

Shopping in Hamiltonhill
Second city of shopping? Not in Hamiltonhill, anyway.
Ian R Mitchell

St Andrew's Halls
The scene of many political meetings, none more significant than that between Lloyd George
and the delegates of the Clyde Workers' Committee in 1915, provoked by the Dilution Crisis.
Ian R Mitchell

Bridgeton Cotton Mill
The massive remains of the Carstairs Street cotton mill in Bridgeton.
Ian R Mitchell

Luma Works SCWS
The gorgeous art deco of the Co-op showing off at its lightbulb factory at Shieldhall, contrasts with the Edwardian grandeur of the main door of the North British Locomotive Company offices in Springburn. Both buildings are still in use, but no longer for industrial purposes.
Ian R Mitchell

North British Locomotive Company offices, Springburn
Ian R Mitchell

Salmon's Savings Bank
Possibly the most ornate doorway in Glasgow. The carvings, ironwork and mosaics of Salmon's Savings Bank in Anderston.

Ian R Mitchell

Tennent's Tenement
Tenement near Tennent's Brewers, showing brewers' tools relief. It housed Tennent's workers.

Ian R Mitchell

Saracen Fountain, Saracen Ironworks, 1901
A masterpiece from the Saracen Ironworks.
The 1901 Empire Exhibition fountain in
Alexandra Park.
Ian R Mitchell

Shipyard Workers, Govan, Pittendrigh
MacGillivray, circa 1880s
The Shipwright and *The Carpenter*, done
by MacGillivray for the main door of the
Fairfield's offices in the 1880s. The offices
are derelict, but the sculptures are still
there, as is – on a much reduced scale –
the shipyard itself.
Ian R Mitchell

Old tobacco factory
Façade of former Players Cigarette Factory on 'Tobacco Road' (Alexandra Parade).
Ian R Mitchell

Old Gorbals
Re-clad 1960s tower blocks loom over the Southern Necropolis.
Ian R Mitchell

St George and the Dragon
Mossman's sculpture of St George and the Dragon at the foot of Maryhill Road. Formerly it
topped the St. George's Cross Co-op building.

Ian R Mitchell

Law Office in Dennistoun
The darker side of Dennistoun. A legal office with an optimistic message.

Ian R Mitchell

Swann's *Views of Glasgow*, plate 17. *The Broomielaw from the South*, 1828.
The widened and deepened River Clyde is already the home to
steam shipping, as well as traditional sail.
Glasgow City Council (Mitchell Library)

externally, and by having a variety of sizes of living space internally. The house interiors featured marble fireplaces and elaborate cornicing, as well as other features. The houses were occupied by solid middle-class people, and many of them had indwelling servants. From their windows over the quarter-century following construction, they saw as much change as I myself have done, though possibly they viewed it with less enthusiasm.

The industrialisation of Glasgow moved west, a huge railway marshalling yard was built to the south of the Crescent, and the planned larger prestige housing development dropped. By 1864, when Thomas Sulman went up in a balloon to draw his *View of Glasgow*, the Crescent is shown surrounded by industrial development, although the docks had not yet been built. The enclave rapidly became hemmed-in by factories and tenement properties, and began a gradual decline. By the 1950s the Crescent was blighted by business/office usage and multiple occupancy. Ladies of commercial affection also used flats in the street. My own flat had been previously tenanted by travelling people, a room to a family. Upstairs was a Robin Hood-type amiable outlaw, who specialised in stripping the lead off neighbouring roofs, while across the landing from him an old lady, spinstered by the First World War, sat amongst her antiques and played the spinnet as a reminder of the street's fashionable origins.

As late as 1970 plans were afoot to demolish the whole area (part of the flanking entrance to Minerva Street was actually demolished). However, times changed. People began to see the attractions of living off-city-centre, off-West-End, and moved in, and a fight led to restoration in the 1980s, instead of demolition – and the granting of A-listed architectural status. One delight of the street is that it must have the highest concentration of bowling greens in the world; three line its southern side, leaving an open outlook to the changing river-front, and sounds of bowls clicking on a summer's evening. One of these greens presents a cameo in its gate, in the form of a fine example of Saracen Foundry cast iron from 1860, made when this works lay nearby in Anderston.

Because of its rollercoaster history the Crescent is possibly the most socially mixed area in Glasgow. Many famous people live or have lived in the Crescent, including John Cairney, Jimmy MacGregor, Daniella Nardini; and it attracts freelance artists, writers and the semi-bohemian alike. But the Crescent also has many working-class residents who moved in when it had lost its earlier middle-class status (our close had a BP oil executive and a North Sea roustabout living in it at the same time), and in the street there are sheltered housing and housing association properties. As a contrast to this, we also had a viscount (impoverished)! Living here is great fun, and has provided a social education in one street for my son. All human life is definitely here! Round the corner in Argyll Street it is colourful, *vif* and multi-cultured (some of the shop fronts could be from Bengal). In the riot of innercity wildlife of the human variety lies the Argyll Street Ash, which now towers above the four-storey tenement building in whose front garden it is rooted – Glasgow's most famous tree. And unlike the one on the city's coat of arms, this one grew!

Heading back down Argyll Street to Anderston proper, you pass at No 1125 the oldest remaining building in the district, a cottage-like structure. This was a former inn on the road from Glasgow to

Partick, and probably dates from the early eighteenth century. Rob Roy was said to use it in his droving days, for an overnight stop, and reputedly had his favourite drinking cup kept for his personal use. We have already seen how, when he stooped to less honourable pursuits such as blackmail, Rob fell out with Menteith of Anderston. In those days Stobcross Mansion stood where the SECC now is and between were fields where Anderstonians grazed their cattle. The inn was in all probability a drovers' stance. It ceased to trade in 1902 and became first a cabinetmakers works and latterly a glass bevelling workshop. It was used for the television production of Roddy Macmillan's play, *The Bevellers*, in the 1980s. MacMillan, celebrated for his TV roles in *Para Handy* and *Daniel Pyke*, was born in Cranston Street, Anderston, and worked for some time as a glass beveller, possibly in that very shop.

In some ways Anderston has been a barometer of Glasgow's fate. Starting as a textile centre it moved into heavy engineering, and then into service and unskilled work, in each case in advance of the city's working-class districts as a whole. There is little doubt it fell far, and even less that it deserved better from the planners who ravaged it. But like the city as a whole, Anderston is slowly recovering, and one hopes that the newcomers to its upmarket peripheries familiarise themselves with its brief civic motto: *Alter alterius auxilio veget* – 'One flourishes with the help of the other'. No man is an island – even in a riverside penthouse. I'm sure Wee Matt, whom we met at the start of this chapter, would agree.

Maryhill

CHAPTER NINE

Maryhill Unlocked

IN A FOLLOWING chapter I suggest that Springburn might be considered the Rome of Glasgow. If the Dear Green Place has a Venice then it has to be Maryhill. Such a designation will surprise the hordes of commuters from Milngavie who rush the three miles down Maryhill Road to Central Glasgow each day, leaving nothing behind but the pollution from their cars for the local weans to inhale. These car-bound souls have possibly never set foot on *terra firma* between Canniesburn Toll and St George's Cross, the beginning and the end of Maryhill Road. But they are the losers.

Anyone with a bit of knowledge of Maryhill will probably be aware that I am suggesting that it is its position astride the nub of Central Scotland's canal system, where the Forth and Clyde Canal joins the route to Port Dundas in Glasgow, that renders Maryhill the Scottish Venice. It also had its Maryhill Fleet – as its conglomeration of boats at Maryhill Dock was affectionately known – as a rival to the maritime might of the former Doges of Venice. (Ironically, as Maryhill and its industry declined, the term 'Maryhill Fleet' was taken over by one of the gangs which briefly flourished in the area.)

But a minimum of two pieces of evidence is required to make a case, and Maryhill has at least such, in that, like Venice, it was also the centre of the glass industry. Indeed Murano Street, overlooking a canal as important as any in Venice, was named after the Italian city's main glass manufactory. In addition Maryhill was the location of one of the most unusual and interesting collections of stained glass in Scotland (*infra*). And then, like Venice with its St Marks, Maryhill had a cathedral. For a while after the Disruption of 1843, the Free Kirkers met in a canalside sawmill at Kelvin Dock with planks for pews, and the place was dubbed 'Maryhill Cathedral'. I rest my case.

Until the Forth and Clyde Canal came along, there was very little thereabouts apart from the rural estates of several leading Glasgow families – and some light industry such as paper-making along the

River Kelvin. But the Kelvin was soon superseded by the canal, the triumph of the latter symbolised by the mighty Kelvin Aqueduct, built between 1787 and 1790, which carried the canal haughtily over the river on four heavy masonry arches. The Kelvin's water-powered mills were also superseded by the clatter of steam engines as industries migrated to the banks of the new waterway.

The Kelvin Aqueduct was a wonder of the world, perhaps the mightiest aqueduct built since Roman times, and tourists flocked to see it, including crowned heads of Europe. It was the technical key to the Forth and Clyde Canal, itself the artery of the first phase of Scotland's Industrial Revolution. The engineer in charge of its construction was Robert Whitworth, and the cost of the structure, at £8,500, almost bankrupted the company building the canal. Scheduled as an Ancient Monument, were this structure in some rural retreat it would be visited by thousands; I doubt if more than a handful of the curious come to see it today. But this may change with the recent reopening of the Forth and Clyde Canal, and the aqueduct could again become a major tourist attraction.

Maryhill was a wild place in the early years of the Industrial Revolution, and an area of the town consisting of lodging houses and public houses was known as the Botany (*Butney* in local parlance and today commemorated in a greasy-spoon joint called The Butney Bite). This area was possibly so-called as it produced so many souls destined for transportation to Botany Bay. The formation of the first Temperance Society in the world in Maryhill in 1824 by John Dunlop apparently did little to curb excessive drinking (it was a fairly lenient organisation in that it pledged abstinence from spirits, but allowed beer and wine). The nature of the work in constructing the canals, and then the railways, and then later still the waterworks to Glasgow from Loch Katrine though the area, meant that large numbers of navvies were drawn to Maryhill. When these overrefreshed themselves, the local Irish priest would enter the hostelries with a shillelagh, and beat about his compatriots until they left the pub. This was dramatic but insufficient law enforcement, and when Glasgow refused to supply a couple of policemen, locals felt they had to act, and police powers were sought – often the main motive for acquiring burgh status. These were attained in 1856 and the town took its name from combining the forename and surname of a wife of the proprietor of a local estate.

These police powers may have helped clean up the town of undesirable aliens, but new dangers soon arose, from within Maryhill, and Glasgow itself. The city council condemned the 'inadequate provision now made for the preservation of the Public Peace in this City on those occasions of Riot and Tumult which too frequently occur in the manufacturing and populous districts from a temporary stagnation in trade and want of employment of the working classes'. Despite the fact that Maryhill was an independent burgh, it agreed to the erection of Glasgow's new barracks, which were moved to Maryhill from the East End. The greatly enlarged complex was opened in 1876.

Mainly locally recruited, and the base of the Highland Light Infantry (HLI) from 1920, the soldiers at Maryhill Barracks were deemed to be unreliable during the 1919 40-hour general strike in Glasgow, and were confined to barracks while troops from elsewhere were brought in to re-impose order. The barracks gave Maryhill the air of a military town; there was a Soldiers' Hotel where those on leave could entertain relatives, and military pubs such as the HLI (now gone) and the Elephant and Bugle (the HLI emblem). Much of the wall of the barracks remains, as does the gatehouse, which gives entry to the Wyndford housing estate which replaced it. The Barracks may not be the Venice *Arsenale*, but the locals were so attached to the gatehouse that they thwarted plans to demolish it. The Soldiers' Hotel became the Maryhill Trades Union Centre for a while and boasts a mural of the whipping of the leader of the 1797 Weavers' Strike through Glasgow. But Maryhill has its own working-class martyr.

In 1834 there was a strike in the calico printing works. The printers replied to the introduction of blackleg labour by sabotage, destroying their work by tearing it or pouring dye on it. The mill manager was entering the works one day when a pile of bricks and a window frame fell near him. They 'maun jist hae tumbl't oot themsel's,' said the strikers. Arrests were made, some workers jailed and troops from Glasgow Barracks were quartered in the works, where the scabs lived and ate for the duration of the strike.

The authorities were then faced with the murder of a striker in the Butney by 'Clay Davie', a nab or nob (blackleg). The police investigation was carried out, but the murderer was discharged. The Calico Printers' Union erected a memorial to the worker in Maryhill Churchyard; an iron pillar with a brass inscription:

TO THE MEMORY OF GEORGE MILLAR, who was mortally wounded at the age on Nineteen on the 24ᵗʰ February 1834, by one of those put to the Calico Printing Trade for the purpose of destroying a Union of the regular workmen, formed to protect their wages. THIS MONUMENT WAS ERECTED BY HIS FELLOW OPERATIVES.

Many of the graves in the churchyard were desecrated by the over-enthusiastic demolition squad, who flattened them into the general rubble when the church itself was demolished, but Millar's was put into storage. It is hoped that Millar's monument might find a home within the former Maryhill Burgh Halls, now awaiting restoration.

Two years after the barracks opened, so did the Municipal Burgh Halls, designed in a revivalist French Renaissance style by David McNaughtan. Maryhill has not the richness of public buildings that areas like Govan or Bridgeton possess, so it is fitting that its municipal buildings are amongst the finest of all the burghs absorbed by Glasgow. Or were the finest, for shortly after celebrating the centenary of Maryhill's annexation by Glasgow, the halls were closed. So too was the swimming pool whose marvellous exterior, stretching back from the Burgh Halls, gives some idea of its former grandeur.

The crowning glory of the Burgh Halls was a series of 20 stained-glass windows made by the Glasgow firm of Stephen Adam. These windows commemorate the industries of Maryhill, and the men and women who worked in them. This in turn gives us the key to Maryhill, its industrial diversity. Govan was ships, Springburn was locomotives, Bridgeton was textiles followed by heavy engineering, but Maryhill had a varied industrial base, recorded in these windows. One of the panels, appropriately enough, commemorates the skills of the glassblower. Another, showing workers in the chemical industry, can be seen in the Glasgow People's Palace. The rest are in the care of the City Council, and depict blacksmiths, carpenters, a gasworker, engineers and many other occupations. This is a unique collection of world historic significance, on a par with Maryhill's other great asset, the Kelvin Aqueduct.

Despite its character as an industrial city, public art in Glasgow largely ignores labour as a theme. Where it is recorded, labour is most often represented by classical maidens as at the Stock Exchange, or by Mossman's medievalised workers on the City Chambers, or even by cherubim operating machinery. Adam's Maryhill stained-glass panels are a dramatic exception, but there are others. MacGillivray's ship-yard workers outside the Govan yard and Lavery's mural of shipyard workers inside the City Chambers spring to mind (see Chapter 4).

The swimming baths have been long closed, so any of the folk of Maryhill desirous of a swim (and not fancying the canal) must find their way to Scotstoun, several miles away. There are no other public sports facilities in Maryhill, none. Plans for redevelopment of the Burgh Halls include the restoration of the swimming pool, an art-space, lifestyle café and business units.

The closure of works like Bryant and May, which provided sports facilities (including a quoits pitch) for their workers, has further encouraged a sedentary lifestyle. But some try. Maryhill FC engage in a sport bearing some resemblance to football, and have produced such greats as Danny McGrain from their ranks – though the last time they won the Junior Cup was in 1940. The Maryhill Harriers still operate, and, though like the Juniors their great days are in the past, they have produced three Olympic competitors, and a marathon gold medallist at the first Empire Games in 1930, 'Dunkie' Wright. The most popular sport amongst the locals would appear to be fishing in the canal. I asked one if he ever caught anything and whether it was fit to eat. 'Oh aye,' he said, 'Ah get a lot o pike. Bit ah never eat it. Ah hate fish'.

In his interesting little book *Memories of Maryhill*, Roderick Williamson tells of his interwar childhood, growing up in Braeside Street, amongst the respectable working classes, adding that gangs, violence and criminality were markedly absent from this area of No Mean City – as was sectarianism. Many of the local men were skilled tradesmen with the council, and Wilkinson's father was unique in being an often-unemployed shipwright – and fervent communist. This was the most respectable part of Maryhill, at the very edge of the historical burgh and bordering on posh North Kelvinside. Jock Nimlin, the greatest of the working-class Glasgow mountaineers, also came from hereabouts. His family were Finnish immigrants, Methodists and ILP members, and Jock worked in the shipyards for many years, before writing and radio work led to a job with the National Trust. Let's start here, for just across Maryhill Road is Charles Rennie Mackintosh's Queen's Cross Church, built in 1899 and the only church Mackintosh designed that was actually built. Today it is the headquarters of the Mackintosh Society, and is open to visitors at certain times.

As you proceed northwards up Maryhill Road you can understand why churches like Queen's Cross were closed, for between here and the junction with Queen Margaret Drive much of the original housing has been demolished, to be replaced by 'landscaped' areas. Signs are, however, that living beside the canal is now being seen as a plus, and new apartments are being built along its banks. From Queen Margaret Drive to Ruchill Street, Maryhill Road retains its original unbroken tenement line, and Ruchill Street itself has a Mackintosh connection, in that the Church Halls, where you can drop in for a cup of tea and a keek, are his work – though not the church itself.

Further up the road we are in the heart of present-day Maryhill, with the site of the barracks on the left. Their wall is now overtowered by the multi storey flats which replaced it, and just a little further on is the Burgh Hall itself, sadly cut off from the community by the closure of Gairbraid Avenue, and of course, the Hall's own closure. The main other building of note hereabouts is the public library on the right side of Maryhill Road, built in 1905, as were so many others in Glasgow, with help from Andrew Carnegie. It has fine sculptures and a separate entrance for Boys and Girls. Passing under an aqueduct which carries the canal over the road you come to the part of Maryhill most associated with the waterway.

On the left are soon seen Maryhill docks, locks and dry dock – with the associated Kelvin Aqueduct – one of the biggest complex of canal construction associated with the entire feat of engineering a canal across Scotland. Still standing too is The White House, a pub dating from the days of canal construction. However, a canalbank hotel built for those using the waterway, which had a 24-hour licence to deal with the constant canal traffic, has gone. The reopening of the canal will, hopefully, be a focus for the regeneration of the whole area around Maryhill Locks, the condition of which is a far cry from that around Queen's Cross where we started. The White House in particular, a graffiti-sprayed eyesore, only needs restoration to re-emerge as a cameo to grace the canalbank.

On 26 May 2001 a fleet of 40 vessels sailed from Falkirk to Bowling, ceremonially reopening the canal. Now holiday operators are offering barge cruises from Glasgow to Falkirk – or all the way to Edinburgh. This is a revival of the use the folk of Maryhill tradition-ally put the canal to. Their 'doon the watter' was a cruise, in boats like the *Gypsy Queen* which ran from 1905 to 1940, along the canal to Kilsyth or further, with jazz bands playing. Until the closure of the canal in 1962 the weans of Maryhill would help the yachtsmen and fishermen, who latterly frequented it, to open the various lock gates, and as reward hitch a lift as far as Clydebank or even Bowling. It is unlikely, however, that any hitched a lift on the midget submarine which negotiated the canal in 1952.

Maryhill Dock is a good point to transfer from Maryhill Road to the canal banks, and retrace steps south, ending up almost where we started. Landscaped, cleaned up and devoted to leisure pursuits, the canal still shows the evidence of its past as the industrial artery of Scotland, and of Maryhill in particular. The economic life of the burgh was so varied that pointing out a few of the more prominent factories, or their remains, is the best policy. The locks at Maryhill had a dock-slipway, still visible, where boat building took place between 1857 and 1921. The firm of Swan built many of the famous Clyde 'Puffers', the iron-hulled and steam-propeller-driven vessels which plied the canal and the Firth of Clyde, including the very first one, the *Glasgow*. The dock is still commemorated in a pub opposite (its tenement gone), called The Kelvin Dock. Swan, who became the first Provost of Maryhill, recruited many of his skilled men from amongst Falkirk's ironworkers. As the canal snakes towards Glasgow, the main branch heads from the Stockingfield Junction towards Falkirk. A confused jumble of buildings now occupies the ground of the former Kelvin, later Maryhill, Iron Works, behind which lies the stadium – if that is not too grand a statement – of Maryhill FC. As you proceed, there is a culvert on your right leading water from the canal to the site of the former works.

On the left now appears the former Bryant and May factory, which produced Scottish Bluebell matches until 1981, and which itself was formerly Alexander Fergusson's Lead and Colour Works. This handsome building, now fronted by a rather faded mural about the delights of the canal, has been converted to non-industrial use. Passing the bascule bridge over the canal at Ruchill Street, you have Mackintosh's Ruchill Halls in view again on the right, while on the left is the site of what was Maryhill's largest industrial undertaking, McLellan's Rubber Works, dating from 1876. With the remains of its own canalside wharfs, and working till a few years ago, the factory is now rubble and ruins, and being redeveloped for housing.

The canal bends, and soon, on the opposite side where now only coots and swans survey the doings of the coarse anglers by the canal banks, are the sites of the two Maryhill glass factories, the Caledonia Works producing bottles and jars, and the Glasgow Works manufacturing plate glass. Much of this land is now taken up by Glasgow University student village. Though Murano Street overlooks the glassworks no more, the canalside here still hosts an active industrial unit in McGhee's Bakery, on the site of the former Firhill Sawmills. The underpassing of the delightfully restored Nolly Brig brings you to Firhill Basin.

On the other side of the canal, within the Ruchill section of the former burgh, are more remains of Maryhill's industrial past. The ironworks of Shaw and MacInnes survived miraculously until the year 2000, and next to that, also on the canal, were found the Phoenix chemical works, not alas rising from the ashes like the mythical bird they were named after. Both works long used the Firhill Basin to transport their products from Maryhill to market. Shaw and MacInnes had originally, like the Swans at Kelvindock, brought their skilled ironworkers from Falkirk; appropriately they came by the canal.

One can take a short walk up to Ruchill Park for a fine view of the city, from its high point, created by building a mini-mountain from the rubble left after the construction of Ruchill Hospital. This, formerly the highest point in Glasgow, used to be known as 'Ben' Whitton, after the then Director of Parks. Or simply head back down to Queen's Cross Church and our starting point at Burnside Street. By

Muirhead Bone *Glasgow; Fifty Drawings* (1911)
The Canal at Maryhill, Plate 48
A sylvan interlude, when the canal at Maryhill was a
semi-rural setting and the lockkeepers kept cows.
Glasgow City Council (Museums)

now you will have a good idea of where the inspiration for those
stained-glass windows in the Burgh Hall came from. And will understand how the Forth and Clyde Canal gave birth to Maryhill.
Hopefully in its new-found role as a tourist, wildlife and recreation
corridor, the waterway will make a contribution towards Maryhill's
regeneration – though the industries of the papermaker, glassblower,
chemical worker and all the others have disappeared forever from the
canal banks.

Possil

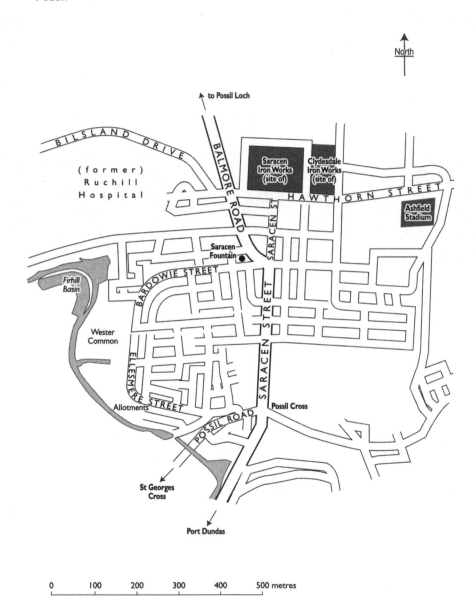

North

to Possil Loch

BILSLAND DRIVE

(former)
Ruchill
Hospital

BALMORE ROAD

Saracen
Iron Works
(site of)

Clydesdale
Iron Works
(site of)

HAWTHORN STREET

SARACEN ST.

Ashfield
Stadium

Saracen
Fountain

BARDOWIE STREET

Firhill
Basin

SARACEN STREET

Wester
Common

ELLESMERE STREET

Allotments

POSSIL ROAD

Possil Cross

St Georges
Cross

Port Dundas

| 0 | 100 | 200 | 300 | 400 | 500 metres |

CHAPTER TEN

Possil Potemkin

A METEORITE FELL on Possil in 1804. Nothing much had happened there before that, and little was to happen for a while thereafter. It is true that the Forth and Clyde Canal had snaked past High Possil at Lambhill in the 1790s, and after curling its way west through Maryhill, turned east and reached Port Dundas, in Low Possil, a decade or so later. But the three miles between Lambhill and Port Dundas remained a rural area till well into the nineteenth century, with not even a village existing.

Ordnance Survey maps of the 1860s show Possil, then in Lanarkshire, as an area of scattered farms, with some quarries and coal pits with attendant miners' rows. Amongst a few country houses the most important was Possil House, built in 1710, and attached to which was much of the land hereabouts. Possil briefly became a point on the literary circuit of Europe, when the lease of Possil House was taken in 1835 by Archibald Allison, a senior member of the Scottish judiciary. He held it till his death in 1867. Born in England of Scottish parents, Allison practised law in Scotland and was involved in many famous trials, from that of Burke the murderer at the beginning of his career to that of Madeleine Smith towards its end. He became Rector of Glasgow University in 1852.

Allison had literary ambitions and wrote a multivolume *History of Europe*, published over a long period, and much of it written at Possil House. Largely unread today this was a bestseller at its time, each volume eagerly awaited, and it sold 100,000 copies in Britain and America, as well as being translated into German, French and Arabic. Possil House became a place of pilgrimage, and royalty from Europe, as well as literati including Charles Dickens, made it a port of call on their trips to Scotland. Allison apparently told Dickens that he had no future as a novelist and should try some other field of literary activity. Visitors found Possil as delightful as did Allison himself. He wrote in his *Autobiography*:

I was fortunate enough to find Possil House unoccupied and to let furnished; it proved a delightful residence. Situated in a park of 30 acres studded with noble trees, some two centuries old.

Allison also enjoyed his daily walk of three miles each way into Glasgow and back, where he continued to engage in public life; indeed he walked to Hamilton and back shortly before his death.

Allison's residence at Possil was not completely trouble-free. He had been involved in the prosecution of the cotton spinners in 1838, a show trial that does little credit to his reputation for impartiality (see the chapter on Anderston), and like many of his time and class was worried by the rebellious condition of the working classes. When, in the year of Chartist agitation of 1842, the local miners went on strike, Allison armed his servants and expected Possil House to be attacked. A message from the miners assured him that he was safe. This did not teach Allison much humanity and he imposed savage sentences of transportation on the alleged ringleaders of the Glasgow 'Chartist' Riots in 1848. On his death in 1867 the Possil estate with the mansion house was put up for sale, and the area was to change dramatically.

Walter Macfarlane had been born in Torrance a few miles north of Possil, but moved to Glasgow and became engaged in the iron-founding trade. At first he set up a foundry in Saracen Street in Calton, but shifted to Anderston in the 1860s as he expanded. There was an insatiable demand for cast-iron goods in the later nineteenth century. Pipes and drains were needed for the expanding programme of sanitation, both domestic and public, parks looked for cast-iron fountains to embellish them, and cast iron was used for decoration on buildings in the form of railings, balconies, and canopies. Soon Macfarlane's works at Anderston were too cramped, for the one thing the casting of iron needs is a huge floorspace. Macfarlane bought the Possil estate in 1868, and decide to establish what we would now call a greenfield site and garden suburb for his workers.

Macfarlane lived in a magnificent house in Glasgow's Park Circus and, having no need for Possil House, he demolished it, though it is commemorated today in Mansion Road. The new foundry was built in two years and opened in 1870, covering a site of 14 acres. Its frontage was an elaborate design featuring much cast iron. Macfarlane built canopies for banks, and botanical gardens, as well as railway stations, specialising in large-scale construction works at the top end of the market. Central Station in Glasgow, where he built the canopy for carriages, is possibly his best local work, and many of the park fountains in the city (see Chapter 12) are his. His nephew of the same name took over the business on his uncle's death in 1885, and by the 1890s 1,200 men were labouring in the Saracen. It was world-famous, its 2,000-page two-volume catalogue a work of art in itself, listing 6,000 items available from the foundry. *Macfarlane's Castings* has recently been republished in a limited edition by a fine art society in the US. The Saracen gained orders from Valparaiso to Vancouver.

Macfarlane was politically prominent in Glasgow, helping found the Liberal Association in 1879, and becoming a firm supporter of Gladstone's reforming policies. He died leaving a personal fortune of £100,000. Interestingly his nephew, in changing times, became a Liberal Unionist, opposing Gladstone's policy of Home Rule for Ireland. Macfarlane was an art collector at his home in Park Circus, which his nephew extensively remodelled in a late high Victorian style. This building is used today for the Glasgow Registry Offices. The house features much cast-iron work, including the elaborate conservatory to the rear made by Macfarlane himself.

From almost nothing Possilpark's population had grown to 10,000 by the 1890s, but this was not solely due to Macfarlane. Possil became the centre for iron founding, and had no fewer than five operating foundries before 1914. The Clydesdale Iron Works stood just east of the Saracen works. These two sites now are occupied by a clutter of garages, warehouses and retail units on Hawthorn Street. To the south in Denmark Street were the Keppoch Iron works and the Possil Iron Works, their demolished sites still vacant. And to the north, at the canal at Strachur Street were the Lambhill Iron Works, which also employed about 1,000 men. But these other works were largely involved in the mass production of cheaper castings, and it was the Saracen which raised cast-iron work to an art form, and whose reputation deservedly survives. It is possible that the proximity of the canal, bringing pig iron from Lanarkshire, was the reason for Possil becoming the centre of the cast-iron industry, or possibly Macfarlane's success there just encouraged others to follow.

Some other interesting industries came to Possil, such as the Nautilus Pottery Works, whose fine ware is now collectible. They closed in 1948. The Workshops for the Blind opened in 1927, but have also since departed. But Possil was basically a foundry town and it prospered while the demand for cast iron was insatiable. However tastes changed, and the fashion for ornate cast iron did not survive the First World War. Later, other materials came along, like plastics for piping, which were cheaper, lighter and more durable. Significantly Lambhill Iron Works closed as early as 1920. The others continued, struggling to adapt and being helped by rearmament work during World War Two. But, constantly reducing in scale, the industry finally died in the 1960s, and the Saracen closed in 1965, five years short of its centenary. Possil suffered. Possil was known originally as a high-wage area with good-quality housing, and even between the wars the overspill areas from its core, such as Hamiltonhill, boasted quality corporation dwellings. Today Possil is one of the areas of the city most ravaged by unemployment, poverty and drugs.

But let that not discourage us, and let us follow, in reverse, the rough route of Sheriff Allison's daily perambulation from Possil to Glasgow and back. On the route north you pass St George's Cross, an area much improved of recent years, where modern flats in the new Glasgow style are mixed with restored Victorian tenements, boldly balustraded. One building, which sadly did not survive redevelopment was a Co-operative Society tenement, which carried a magnificent sandstone statue of St George and the Dragon by Mossman. This statue is now the centrepiece of a landscaped seating area, which, however, could do with better maintenance and cleaning.

St George's Road is a study in contrasts; alongside some of the highest multistorey blocks in Glasgow are dotted little cameos of the past, an old town house, and St George's in the Fields, a fine Victorian church now also flatted. Further on still, Possil Road goes under a rather forbidding canal aqueduct, so let's take the scenic route to Possil. Heading up the remaining granite setts of Baird's Brae you come to the towpath of the branch of the Forth and Clyde Canal which leads to Port Dundas. From the later eighteenth century until closure in the 1950s, this was a port for much of Glasgow's trade, especially for the distilleries roundabouts, and at Spiers Wharf are what must be the most splendid warehouses on earth, like Adam mansions, now mainly converted into flats. Swans nest where the barges once emptied their cargoes of grain.

At the canal footbridge are the offices of the British Waterways Board, with a collection of aquatic craft moored at Possil Basin. On the opposite bank of the canal is a huge wild area, a sight of scenic beauty, give or take a few wrecked cars and supermarket trolleys. You discover the method of gaining access to this wild area, and make other discoveries in the process, when you cross the canal bridge and head up Applecross Street for Hamiltonhill, moving along Ellesmere Street.

Glasgow may aspire to be Britain's second shopping city now, but not here, not in Hamiltonhill where four of the six shops in the local shopping centre are closed, boarded up and for let. How do people here purchase the necessities of life? One possible answer is given by the allotments on Ellesmere Street, still bravely tended and producing vegetables – and social interaction. The guys working there were quite willing to chat and show me around. 'It's no sae much for the vegetables, we gie maist of them away. It's tae pass the time and get oot the hoose,' said one of my hosts. On a recent visit I found these allotments deserted and overgrown. The site was closed due to fears of soil contamination. Tests are being carried out, and hopefully the allotments will be allowed to re-open. Another surprise lies further on at Westercommon, whose location was indicated by a just-legible fire-damaged sign. Braving the entrance, which was cunningly camouflaged to look like a rubbish coup, I entered. The common has the best view of Glasgow from anywhere, one to die for; the city looks like Florence – well, a wee bit – with the Italianate towers of Park Circus in the middle foreground.

Westercommon is what is left of Glasgow's once extensive common lands, where inhabitants had the right to graze cattle, which were driven out through Cowcaddens to pasture. The city's population also had the right to quarry building stone and collect turf and wood for fuel. From the Clyde at Partick these lands stretched to Possil, but much was sold off to pay Glasgow's debts in the eighteenth century, after the Shawfield Riots of 1725 against the malt tax. In clashes with troops eight rioters had been killed at the Shawfield Mansion in Glasgow. This was the home of Duncan Campbell, MP for the city, and supposedly a supporter of the malt tax. The government wanted the council to take action against the rioters, but instead the baillies started to proceed against the military authorities for murder. Some council members were arrested when General Wade, no less, was sent to the city to restore order.

The Glasgow authorities' ill-disguised support for these riots against the malt tax led to a heavy fine being imposed on the city, while many rioters were flogged, imprisoned or banished. In subsequent rather shady deals, the Glasgow city authorities somewhat undermined their heroic stand over the Shawfield Riots. After paying the fine through the sale of the common lands, most of what was left was divided up between the grasping baillies for nominal sums. All that remains now is several acres of wild land sloping down to the canal. And the malt tax.

I was glad to see that the citizens of Glasgow are still insisting on their common rights, at least here in Hamiltonhill. Apart from using it as a place for building their corrugated iron pigeon lofts, modern versions of the old Scottish dookit, and as an unofficial kids' scramble bike track, the locals have made Westercommon into a museum of old furniture, cars and kitchen appliances, awaiting a refuse van which never comes. Nevertheless here is a wetland, a reeded habitat by the canal supporting a great variety of waterfowl, swans, coots, widgeon and tufted duck – and pigeons from the lofts on the bank. Firhill Basin, with the removal of canal bridges, now boasts an artificial island and protected nesting site. An urban forest and wetland in one, and a resource for the local people, very few of whom belong to the car-owning class that can escape easily to the countryside. Access to a car is often used as a poverty index. At one household in ten, Possil's car-access rate is the lowest in the UK.

From Westercommon can be seen to advantage the A-listed tower of the former Ruchill Hospital in Ruchill Park. This was Glasgow's fever hospital, and the grounds are scheduled for a housing development. Its parkland setting and high walls make it an attractive prospect for middle-class housing, aimed at drawing families back to Glasgow. They would have their own school and shopping facilities, and of course, the high wall to keep out undesireables. While this might broaden Glasgow's tax base, what does it do for the supposed policy of social inclusion? On the northern side of the park on Bilsland Drive are some of the grand former residences for doctors and nurses; these have been sold off for private housing, although the former hospital laundry has been made into social housing, as part of the Possil Corridor improvement.

Heading down Ellesmere Street and Bardowie Street towards Saracen Street, you are in the heart of Possil. At the street's north end is a small Macfarlane fountain, with the message 'Keep the Pavement Dry'. I was reflecting that this, and the land for the library, was the sum of Macfarlane's benificence to Possil, when I was interrupted. In Possil of all places, where nobody goes, you are visible as an outsider, but my interest in the fountain probably indicated that I was neither a social security investigator nor, worse still, an arm of the law. Bob and I got quite pally and we went for a drink, at his request, after our chat. It went something like this:

Bob 'Aye, he gave a lot tae Possil did Macfarlane.'
Reply 'But he took a lot mair oot.'
Bob 'You're a smart bugger, eh? Aye, right enough, so he did. Used tae be a great place Possil, but it's got a bad reputation noo, and it deserves it tae. Ah served ma time in the Saracen, but I didnae like it and shifted tae the distillery at Port Dundas. That started ma problems. Ah'm an alcoholic noo. Ye fancy buyin me a pint?'

As we entered the pub I heard one woman shout to another:

'Hey, Jeannie, the Housing Association says ye've tae pit curtains up, in case the kids think yer hoose is unoccupied and fling bricks at the windaes.'

And thus I learned there was an ethical code governing 'daein in windaes' in Possil.

I somewhat scandalised Bob by refusing to join him in a pint at 11.30 am and, after settling him down, carried on with my travels along Saracen Street. At first sight this street is appealing, if lacking in great architectural merit. There are no gap sites, and the shops are occupied, the pubs still there, as is the Co-op building and the Lido 'Tally' Café, much as it would have been 50 to 100 years ago, and there is a healthy bustle. But Saracen Street is like those Potemkin Villages built for Catherine the Great in Russia, which had nothing behind the main street. For to the east and west of Saracen Street lie what must be the most extensive brownfield sites in Glasgow, hundreds of acres of flattened, derelict and overgrown land. A start has been made in building new, low-rise housing, but it is difficult to see where the population will come from to fill these wastes.

There is not a lot to detain the eye in Saracen Street, but it is worth visiting Possil Library. The land was given by Macfarlane, the construction funded by a Carnegie grant, and the building opened in 1913. Its most interesting features are five interior murals done by final-year students of the Glasgow School of Art that year. These represent Geography, Art and so forth and are attractive if conventional. Commerce is, as usual, represented by classical maidens. At the bottom of Saracen Street is Saracen Cross, or rather what is left of it, that is two pubs, and then Craighall Road leads back into town via Port Dundas. Some Possil folk would have worked here in times past as unskilled labourers, and plans to develop the derelict site as a trading estate might bring some work for the local community.

An underused facility in Possil is the loch at High Possil. On the canal here, beside where the Lambhill iron works stood, can also be found a ruined mansion-cum-warehouse, dating from shortly after the canal's construction. A restoration of this listed building would be a good headquarters for Possil Loch which is a Site of Scientific Interest and an important wintering site of wildfowl. The loch is surrounded by boggy ground and thick reeds, and I suspect few Possil folk know it is there; the birds appear undisturbed. But it is a good place to sit and ponder the poblems of Possil on a fine afternoon.

The basic problem in areas like Possil is that a lifestyle has emerged and we are now into its third generation. The grandfathers lost their jobs, the fathers didn't work and now these in turn have produced kids. Unemployment in areas like Possil is probably three times the official figure; to it should be added those on disability benefits, and those, like unmarried mothers, on social security, neither of whom count in the unemployment totals. In Glasgow as a whole 25% of

those of employment age are not working. Either they are unemployed, on sickness or disability benefits, or on social security. In areas
like Possil the figure is safely double or even treble that; here almost
nobody works.

There are no jobs for the people in Possil and they have not the
skills or means to obtain work elsewhere. But they have learned to
survive, on benefits supplemented by the black economy. And the
ones who escape this poverty of ambition are the criminals and drug
dealers. There are no books on Possil, no autobiographies of life there
(since no one famous came from Possil). It doesn't feature in histories
of the city, since even its main industry seems to have been forgotten
in a way that shipbuilding and railway construction have not. Poor
Possil. I feel for it the way I would a scubby stray dug. Let's transpose
to it a refrain originally describing Camlachie, an area which now no
longer exists, and which, despite everything, I'm sure still expresses
the feelings of many of Possil's remaning inhabitants:

Oh Possil, oh Possil, oh Possil my ain
I love each dirty windae, each broken doon stane.

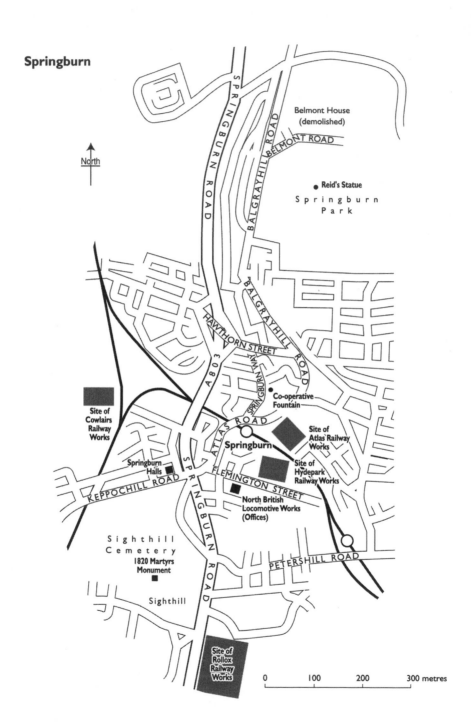

Springburn

North

Springburn

Belmont House
(demolished)

BELMONT ROAD

SPRINGBURN ROAD

BALGRAYHILL

Reid's Statue

Springburn
Park

BALGRAYHILL ROAD

HAWTHORN STREET

SPRINGBURN WAY

A803

Co-operative
Fountain

Site of
Cowlairs
Railway
Works

ATLAS ROAD

Springburn

Site of
Atlas Railway
Works

Springburn
Halls

Site of
Hydepark
Railway Works

KEPPOCHILL ROAD

SPRINGBURN ROAD

FLEMINGTON STREET

North British
Locomotive Works
(Offices)

Sighthill
Cemetery

1820 Martyrs
Monument

PETERSHILL ROAD

Sighthill

Site of
Rollox
Railway
Works

0   100   200   300 metres

CHAPTER ELEVEN

Springburn: Rome of the North

Born Balgrayhill Schooled Petershill
Worked Keppochhill Married Springburnhill
Sick Stobhill Domiciled Barnhill
Rested Sighthill

SPRINGBURN – THE ROME of the North? But consider the evidence. Like Rome, Glasgow's Springburn is built on seven hills, as this ditty records. And the Romans were there – in fact they built the Antonine Wall just to the north of Springburn, and through the area a Roman road went to the fort on the wall at Cadder.

But most tellingly, just as in the days of the Roman Empire when 'all roads led to Rome', so at the height of the British Empire, all roads, or at least the vital iron ones, led to Springburn. The British Empire was held together by its railways, and before 1914 more than half of the locomotives riding the lines of mother country and colonies were built in Springburn. From the workshops there, they trundled down the tramlines at night to the docks, and thence were carried by sea to all parts of the globe. These events were marked by the local population, who poured out under the gas streetlamps, to watch the mighty engines rolling by.

In Springburn Park there stands, like a memorial to a Roman emperor, the statue of James Reid. From the highest hill in Glasgow, he looks down over the district which was his own empire, and whose character he did so much to forge. Born in Auchterarder in 1823, Reid became a partner in, and manager of, the Hydepark Works, which he bought over in 1876, bringing his sons into the business. Before he died in 1894, Reid had left his mark on Springburn – and on Glasgow itself. Springburn Park opened in 1892, and the following year Reid gifted a bandstand, constructed by MacFarlane's Saracen Foundry in Possil, to it. Reid's statue was erected in the park in 1900, and commemorated his role both as President of the Society of Engineers and Shipbuilders, and President of the Royal Glasgow Institute of Fine Arts. The family were art collectors, and a fine portrait of James Reid hangs in Glasgow Kelvingrove Galleries, to which they also gifted a Constable, a Corot and a Turner.

John's son Hugh left an even bigger mark on Springburn, and especially its fine park. He purchased the mansion and grounds of Mosesfield in 1904, and donated these to the park. In Mosesfield mansion in 1896 George Johnston created the prototype of the Arrol–Johnston motor car, and laid the foundation of the Scottish automobile industry. Thus in Springburn, at the height of the boom in the railways, was invented the vehicle that would lead to the sad demise of the iron ways. After a while as Springburn Museum, Mosesfield mansion became an old men's club, which it remains.

His own mansion, Belmont House, was built in 1889 by Hugh Reid on his marriage and in its day was both the largest and the highest (at 350 feet above sea level) house in Glasgow, with a view from its eminence overlooking seven counties. When he died in 1935 he left the building for use as a children's home. Unfortunately, after a while as a training school for nurses and as administrative buildings for Stobhill Hospital, Belmont was demolished in 1985. Other features in the park recalling Hugh Reid are the Unicorn Column, a pottery monument supplied by Doulton of Lambeth; this was originally erected elsewhere but has been in the park since 1970. Its formerly vandalised unicorn has now been restored to the top of the column. Hugh also donated £10,000 in 1900 to the now-derelict but once-magnificent Winter Gardens in the park; there is talk of restoration here. The splendid rockery remains open, however.

In the era when, apart from the summer holiday, most working people found their recreational opportunities limited to the local public park, the area reflected many of the aspects of the social values the upper classes sought to impose on the lower orders. Within the park's bounds, approved uplifting recreational activities took place, as did approved entertainment. They were closed on Sundays and no alcohol was sold. The parks frequently hosted war memorials emphasising the duty of loyalty to King and Country, and statues of civic dignitaries, often local capitalists, recording their benevolence. Springburn Park is a fine example of the park as a value system.

The basis of this Reid family largesse was the enormous wealth generated by locomotive manufacture before 1914. Before air and even road were serious rivals to its transport monopoly, the possession of a worldwide Empire provided a captive market for steam railway engines. Hugh Reid astutely brought about the end of competition between the Glasgow-based locomotive manufacturers in 1903, through an amalgamation of the Hydepark with its main rivals, the Atlas Works and Queen's Park Works, to form the North British Locomotive Works. From being a sleepy weavers' village in the 1840s, Springburn by 1900 was the centre of world locomotive-making, with up to 15,000 people working in the railway factories and associated railway yards.

Springburn's advantages turned into disadvantages. Its factories continued to mass-produce steam locomotives for a diminishing Empire and a diminishing market. The general manager of the NBLC predicted in 1936 that electricity would never replace steam on mainline trains. By the time the Glasgow works switched to diesel, and later electric, locomotives, they were unable to compete. Locomotive production stopped in Springburn in the 1960s. An ever-shrinking BREL repair workshop facility at Cowlairs continued as the area's sole link with its glorious industrial past, until it was closed with the loss of 1,600 jobs in 1986. You can see many fine specimens of Springburn's craftsmanship in the Glasgow Transport Museum.

Unlike some other industrial areas of Glasgow, which were almost entirely working-class, Springburn had a more complex class structure, and Balgrayhill, in which the park was situated, was then the desirable part of Springburn. Aside from Mosesfield mansion and the 'wee hoose above the shop', i.e. Reid's Belmont mansion to the north of the park, the southern park boundary was formed by Broomfield Road, a street of solid middle-class villas. This 'posh' bit of Springburn even has a 'castle' in the form of Balgray Tower. Locally known as Breezes Tower, this is a mock-Tudor house built in the 1830s, with a three-storey central octagonal tower – still functioning as a dwelling house. Urban myths are fascinating. I was studying the tower when a proud local came up and claimed, 'It was built by a tobacco lord, for tae see his ships comin up the Clyde'. I didn't have the heart to point out the tobacco lords were long gone by 1830, and

I left him with his myth. But he was right when he told me, to my initial scepticism, 'And there's a Rennie Mackintosh hoose just doon below it'. At 140–2 Balgrayhill Road is indeed a two-storey semi-detached villa which was designed by Charles Rennie Macintosh in 1890. Its semi-octagonal bay windows with stained glass are all that remain of Macintosh's imprint, however, as the interiors were gutted some time ago. From Balgrayhill the rest of Springburn was, and remains – literally and socially – downhill – though it should be said that in its heyday Springburn was one of the most prosperous and 'respectable' of Glasgow's working-class areas, because of the high proportion of skilled workers employed in the locomotive works.

Tom Weir wrote something about this respectable working-class world of the Springburn, in which he grew up between the wars, in his autobiography, *Weir's World* (1994):

> As a lad I found the noise and stir of Springburn exciting. Each morning an army of locomotive workmen, thousands strong, answered the shriek of the hooters, the noise of their heavy boots clattering on the pavements, all in a uniform of dungarees. Noisy tramcars, bells clanging, would be chuntering up and down Springburn Road, where shops of every kind faced each other, many bearing the logo of Cowlairs Co-operative Society.

Both Tom's parents were from railway working families, and his mother worked as a painter in the locomotive shops for a while. His was the world of the Boy's Brigade, YMCA, cycling and boxing clubs to keep fit, and trips to Springburn Library or even tramps across Glasgow to the Mitchell Library for self-education. Like many mothers, Tom's wanted him to have a white-collar job and on leaving school he started worked in the Co-operative stores. But not desiring to have engraved on his tombstone 'Born a Man, died a Grocer', Tom eventually managed to escape and to earn himself a living as a well-loved broadcaster and writer on the great outdoors, including having a monthly feature in the *Scots Magazine* for many years. One impetus to his outdoor career was that from Springburn's hills you could see the distant, greater hills of the Campsies, and beyond those, Ben Lomond and the mountains of Arrochar.

More than many other areas of Glasgow, Springburn's original street pattern has been obliterated by redevelopment. Dropping down Balgrayhill along Lenzie Street there is almost nothing left of pre-1970s Springburn. Along Springburn Way some of the former buildings stand, but the centre of Springburn now consists mainly of a shopping centre and a sports centre which, though functional, are of limited visual interest or architectural merit. Gone are landmarks like Quinn's Bar with its tower clock and its famous (understairs) howff where favoured regulars could drink after hours, immortalised in the song:

> Doon in the wee room underneath the sterr
> Everybody's happy, everybody's there
> Were a' getting merry each in his cherr
> Doon in the wee room underneath the sterr.

Historic Springburn was literally sliced in half by the construction in the 1970s of the A803 road, the purpose of which was to speed up by a few minutes the daily incoming and exiting of commuters working in Glasgow but living in places like Bishopbriggs – not in Glasgow, absurdly, though most of its inhabitants work in the city. This road, which so damaged Springburn, was not constructed for its inhabitants, since car ownership there is the Glasgow average of about one third of households. It forcibly divided one half of Springburn from its shops and facilities by a dual carriageway with associated overpasses, and the demolition for the road has left us – 30 years later – with large vacant grassed over spaces on each side. As a symbol of this neglect stand (only just!) the formerly glorious Springburn Public Halls, constructed in 1902 – again partly funded by the benefactions of the Reid family. If you look carefully at the façade on their frontage you will see two Greek goddesses, representing Art and Industry (the latter cradling a locomotive). The halls are now the home of broken windows, pigeons and graffiti.

About the only relic hereabouts of Springburn's glory days is the Co-op Fountain, originally erected in 1902 at the Cross, but moved to the shopping centre in 1981. Its motto is 'Unity is Strength' and it recalls the times when the Co-op was a vital part of working-class life. Indeed, the Springburn and Cowlairs Co-op was largely owned by the local railway workers, and was actually founded in 1881 when workers on strike could not get credit from local shopkeepers. It became a roaring success, with 26 branches. Another function of the Co-op was to provide a loan for those having to purchase their tools on taking up a railway apprenticeship.

A little further on from the shopping centre you come to Springburn Station, whose delapidated state is a biting irony, given that Springburn was once the world's railway capital. The Hydepark works lay to the south of the railway line, while the Atlas was situated to the north. The latter factory gives its name to Atlas Square, where the Springburn Library was located till recently. A plaque on the wall commemorates the refurbishing of this and the opening of an associated Springburn Museum by Tom Weir in 1988. The library has recently been moved to the sports centre where there is a small display on the history of Springburn, and where the local History Group meets. The library staff are extremely helpful, and the place has a collection of old pictures and maps worth looking at, and leaflets about Springburn's heritage, including one produced for the 1999 Year of Architecture, on Springburn's various historical monuments.

Springburn was an early centre of trades unionism and socialist groupings. In 1890 the first national strike of railwaymen was centred on Springburn, when 9,000 men came out, largely in protest against the enforced working of excessive hours, sometimes up to 20 per day. The Cowlairs and St Rollox works were actually owned by the railway companies, and their workers joined the strike. Gangs of pickets engaged in nocturnal skirmishes with police in the Springburn streets, and the police report of the strike described the incident thus:

> Shortly after midnight a body of strikers, sixty strong, arrived upon the scene, and proceeded in marching order in the direction of the railway at St. Rollox. A sufficient number of constables having been brought together, the strikers were charged...

It is significant that the Hydepark works, a family-owned firm, did not join the strike. Reid, its owner, was paternalistic and determinedly anti-union. This attitude at Hydepark continued even after it merged with its rivals to form the North British Locomotive

Company, and in the General Strike of 1926, while the other railway workshops came out for the miners, the response at Hydepark was very patchy. (Only in the 1950s with an influx of militant electricians when the works converted to electric trains, did this deferential attitude end at Hydepark.) Generally, though, the strike was solid in Springburn and J Thomas recalls in *The Springburn Story* that a tramcar driven by a volunteer was hounded out of Springburn by flour bombs – despite the pile of stones lying handy from a demolished building. He comments that, 'The Springburn revolutionaries, rather than throw stones, queued up at the local shop to buy flour bombs at their own expense.'

John Paton was an Aberdonian socialist who came to Glasgow before World War One to experience what he called 'the more exciting and wider world' of the big city. He got a job in Springburn as a barber and married there, joining the local ILP. He describes the optimism and activity of that period well, and comments in *Proletarian Pilgrimage* (1936):

> The Springburn ILP was a hive of activity. It had about a hundred members and a steady flow of new recruits. For the most part the men belonged to the skilled trades like engineering, and were almost always known as good and steady workmen. They were active trades unionists to a man. The great majority were total abstainers. There was a strong element of puritanism in their make-up.

Paton's optimism as to the future a century ago – and arrogance about his political correctness – echoes my own on arriving in Glasgow just after the huge class struggles of the early 1970s, and thinking that a new world was at hand. Like most other heavily working-class areas of Glasgow, Springburn returned an ILP Red Clydesider member to Westminster in 1922. Paton stood for the ILP in a couple of seats and failed, becoming in turn national organiser and editor of its paper, *New Leader*. Eventually he moved right and became a Labour MP in the 1945 landslide election. His book remains a wonderful account of a historical period, and deserves to be reprinted.

It is surprising and gratifying that anything of Springburn's heritage has escaped the demolition men or the more insidious effects of neglect, but in Flemington Street you can get a glimpse of former glory. The buildings of the present North Glasgow College were once the offices of the North British Locomotive Company. Outside are fine sculptures representing Science and Speed, while over the front door is the splendid carved elevation of a locomotive. But these fore-tastes are nothing to what lies inside. You could spend hours in here, and there is even a Heritage Trail, which the college encourages visi-tors to follow. Plaques commemorate the dead of both wars who worked for the company, and also the opening of the building by Lord Roseberry in 1908. A magnificent wood and marble staircase leads to the even more magnificent boardroom. The windows behind the staircase contain striking stained-glass World War One memori-als, one of which is a fine portrayal of a female munitions worker at her lathe. She looks sad. Maybe she is mourning one of the 300 men from the NBLC killed in action. The jannie who showed me round is justifiably proud of his building. 'But it's amazing how few people are aware of it, even in Springburn itself,' he commented, 'though we are always willing to show folk round.' Places like this should be on any Glasgow visitor's itinerary.

As Springburn Park is the 'dear green place' in the north of the dis-trict, so Sighthill Cemetery is the same in the south. Sighthill is so called because of the view that can be had from it, and here in the 1840s Glasgow opened up a large new cemetery. Though not having the status of residents of the Necropolis beside Glasgow Cathedral, where Glasgow's *haute bourgeoises* were buried, those interred in Sighthill were nevertheless 'quality': shipmasters, professional men and the like. James Mossman is buried here, beneath a fairly simple stone. Mossman founded the firm (which still exists near Glasgow Cathedral) of monumental sculptors that was responsible for more public sculpture in Victorian Glasgow than any other. Regrettably Ray Mackenzie's wonderful book, *Sculpture in Glasgow* (1999), which does so much for Mossman's reputation, does not include his burial stone in it, nor any of the other fine public sculpture of Springburn. An omission to be corrected, one hopes.

The most famous of those interred at Sighthill were, however, of much lower rank. In 1847 a monument was raised by public sub-

Muirhead Bone *Glasgow; Fifty Drawings* (1911)
St Rollox
The utter desolation of the St Rollox chemical waste mounds inspired this drawing.
Glasgow City Council (Museums)

scription to honour John Baird and Andrew Hardie (later James Wilson was also commemorated there). These three men were all executed for taking part in the so-called Radical War of 1820. In that year the first mass strike in world history took place when 60,000 workers in the West of Scotland downed tools for the right to vote. Baird, Wilson and Hardie, along with some others carried their protest as far as armed insurrection, and paid the ultimate price, though their example inspired later generations of reformers who eventually achieved many of the original aims of the men of 1820.

In *Glasgow and its Clubs*, written in 1856, John Strang quotes from the account of a member of the Waterloo Club, a patriotic organisation, describing the panic that seized the city. The authorities mobilised the soldiers at Bridgeton Barracks and called out volunteer middle-class militias, to defend the city against expected attack. The account states:

From Sunday morning, when the famous or rather infamous inflammatory placard was posted at the corner of the streets, all the public works and factories were closed, while the miners in and around Glasgow struck work.

The volunteer militias patrolled the streets, where 'idle crowds, collected in gloomy groups about the corners of the leading thoroughfares', and the 'ill-conditioned, irritable and starving working men in Calton, Bridgeton and the Gorbals' were on strike. But only scattered risings took place.

From the cemetery you overlook the housing of Sighthill, now home to many asylum seekers fleeing persecution abroad, and reminding us that even today not everyone has the rights and freedoms for which those like Baird and Hardie fought almost two centuries ago. Sighthill has had its tensions over this asylum issue, but indications now are that community relations are improving. Walking around there made me think of the song *Freedom Come All Ye* by the late great Scottish writer Hamish Henderson, whose lines cite his hopes for the future:

When John Maclean meets wi his freens in Springburn
A the roses and geans will turn tae bloom

Black and white ane till ither mairreit
Can find bried, barley bree and painted room

We started this exploration of Springburn with the railway 'Emperor' Reid on his high hill above Springburn. It is fitting that we end also with a railway theme, and just to the east of Sighthill Park, in the area now occupied by the interstices of the M8 and the A803, stood, till 1964, the St Rollox Chemical Works. With Glasgow all industrial history is in superlatives – biggest, first, greatest – and St Rollox is no exception. This was the largest chemical works in Europe, as well as one of the oldest, founded in 1797. Its chimney, known as Tennent's Lum, was, at 435 feet, reputedly the highest in the world and a landmark far and wide until it was demolished in 1922. This was also the site of Scotland's first railway, the Garnkirk to Glasgow, which was constructed in 1831 to supply St Rollox with coal, and was opened by none other than George Stephenson, the railway pioneer. St Rollox also created huge chemical waste deposits, which enjoyed an infamy sufficient for Glasgow artist Muirhead Bone to try to convey the sense of desolation they inspired. Today these wastes lie underneath Sighthill Park and the housing surrounding it.

The largest chemical works in the world, like the largest railway workshops, are found no more in Springburn. Belmont mansion is gone, the Winter Gardens are a skeleton, the Public Hall a rotting shell. Like Rome, the streets of Springburn are filled with ruins and ghosts. But Springburn's time, like that of Rome, may yet come again. However, unlike the Gorbals or Bridgeton, Springburn lies a little too far from booming central Glasgow to benefit from its commercial and housing developments, and it may have to wait a little while for the roses and geans to bloom.

Dennistoun

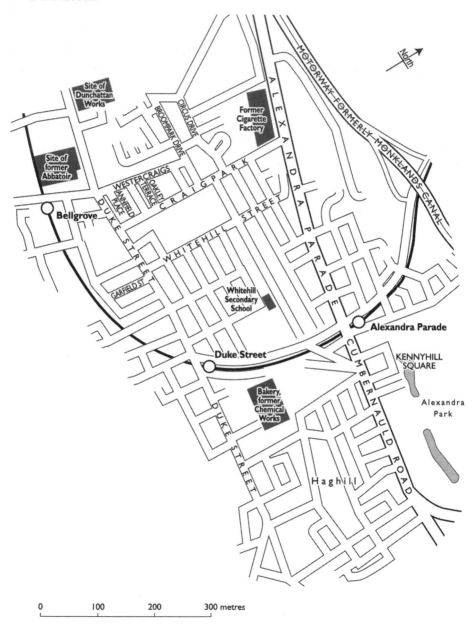

Site of
Dunchattan
Works

Former
Cigarette
Factory

BROOMPARK DRIVE

CIRCUS DRIVE

ALEXANDRA

MOTORWAY-FORMERLY-MONKLANDS-CANAL

North

Site of
former
Abbatoir

WESTERCRAIGS

OAKLEY TERRACE

ANNFIELD PLACE

CRAIGPARK

PARADE

Bellgrove

DUKE STREET

WHITEHILL STREET

GARFIELD ST

Whitehill
Secondary
School

Alexandra Parade

CUMBERNAULD ROAD

KENNYHILL
SQUARE

Duke Street

Alexandra
Park

Bakery,
former
Chemical
Works

DUKE STREET

Haghill

0   100   200   300 metres

CHAPTER TWELVE

Dennistoun: No Mean Streets

THE DISTRICT OF DENNISTOUN is an island. Not only is it physically situated on rising ground above Townhead, Bridgeton and Parkhead, but it was, and remains, socially an island of unfliniching respectability in the surrounding East End of Glasgow. For many working-class folk in that part of the town, Dennistoun was the summit of their social ambitions. While socialist activists on Glasgow Green hoped to lead the working classes to the promised land, most of them would just have settled for Dennistoun.

The Glasgow singer Lulu moved to Dennistoun as a girl from Bridgeton, and said (in her autobiography *I Don't Want to Fight*):

> When we moved from Soho Street across the railway bridge to Garfield Street, it was only a couple of hundred yards, but mentally it was a lot further. We had edged slightly up in the world because we now lived closer to Duke Street and further away from the Gallowgate. There weren't so many poorly dressed kids or runny noses.

Andrew Stewart dedicated a book of photographs of the area, *Old Dennistoun,* to his parents, of whom he says that they 'had one of their hopes fulfilled when we moved house from Townhead to Dennistoun.' Like Lulu, he had moved a very short distance, but into an area that signified an important step up the social ladder. A mark of its social status and respectability is that until the 1960s, in a city renowned for its alcohol abuse, the Dennistoun area was 'dry'.

But had things developed differently, Dennistoun would not be a by-word for working-class respectability, but instead a residential area for the upper and middle classes to rival Glasgow's West End. Alexander Dennistoun was from a Glasgow banking family, and in 1856 he engaged the renowned Victorian architect James Salmon to plan and lay out a residential suburb called after him. Only a few streets were built in the 1860s and 1870s, before the spread of the heavy industries roundabout caused the plan to be aborted. Tucked away between Duke Street and Alexandra Parade, the villas and terraces which remain from Salmon's grand design are one of the little-known treasures of Glasgow.

In 1872 John Tweed's *Guide to Glasgow and the Clyde* had this area very definitely on the tourist itinerary, recommending a walk to 'the pleasant suburb of Dennistoun. It is well laid out and contains many fine villas and lodges. The approach by Alexandra Parade is very fine.'

The area was subsequently feued for the building of tenements from the 1880s, although they were of a quality generally much higher than the rest of the East End. At first these were expected to attract middle-class tenants, but by 1914 Dennistoun had instead become the residential location of the aristocracy of the working class.

And Dennistoun had had another false start before finding its identity, being the location of one of the birthplaces of the Industrial Revolution. In the 1770s George Macintosh, in partnership with David Dale of New Lanark, established a factory in Dennistoun, to the east of the present Necropolis. This was set up to produce cudbear, a dye for the textile industry. As well as the factory Macintosh built a model village for his workers, with housing and educational facilities. The roll call at the Dunchattan works every morning was in Gaelic, for Macintosh employed only Gaelic speakers. The reason for this was not that the Highlanders had a good reputation as hard workers (on the contrary) but that being Gaelic speakers, and being discouraged from communicating with people from outwith the settlement (he even surrounded the factory with a high wall), Macintosh hoped to be able to protect his industrial secrets from competitors.

George's son Charles continued the business and experimented in industrial chemistry, having taken classes with Joseph Black at Glasgow University. He discovered that ammonia, in the form of naptha, a by-product to the making of his cudbear, would dissolve rubber. This gave birth to the waterproofing of textiles, and the dubbing of such garments as 'mackintoshes'. Shortly before his death in 1843, Macintosh moved the works to Manchester and Dennistoun's contribution to industrial progress ceased, for it never again became a centre of industry. This period is however commemorated in the naming of the 1970s and 80s housing at Dunchattan Street and Macintosh Court, on the site of the former works.

After this experiment ended, people tended to live in Dennistoun, but not to work in it. For, unlike many of the other areas of Glasgow where housing and manufacturing were in close proximity, industry was located at the edges of Dennistoun. To the east lay the chemical works, to the south the slaughterhouse, and to the north the steel-works and gasworks, separated from Dennistoun by the Monklands Canal. All firmly outwith the residential streets of the area. Later, Alexandra Parade became the centre of Glasgow's cigarette industry and was awarded the name Tobacco Road. But even there, you were past the factories before you arrived at the tenement buildings. With its lack of industry and its good housing, it is easy to understand why so many in Calton or Camlachie looked enviously uphill at the denizens of Dennistoun.

Dennistoun's position as the area's jewel in the crown was recognised when it was chosen to stage both the East End Industrial Exhibitions; that of 1890–91 and the subsequent one in 1903–4; 750,000 attended the first and over a million the second. The first raised £3,000 for the building of the People's Palace, which many expected would be in Dennistoun's Alexandra Park, but was instead placed on Glasgow Green. The educational exhibits drew crowds, but the main event was the 'Buffalo Bill' Wild West Show, starring Colonel Cody himself. Dennistoun was later to produce many characters in the world of entertainment to rival Buffalo Bill.

Which brings us back to Lulu. Let us start, as she did, with a railway crossing. The train today deposits the traveller at Bellgrove Station and on exiting, to the left is Bridgeton, literally on the wrong side of the tracks. To the right, across the railway bridge which Lulu saw a social marker, is Dennistoun. On crossing Duke Street, and heading up Westercraigs, you are in the heart of what was actually executed of Salmon's plans for a grand suburb. Salmon himself originally lived here, and so too did Sir William Arrol, who opened his Dalmarnock Iron Works in Bridgeton in 1868, and who is best remembered for the construction of the Forth Bridge in 1890. Arrol gave 10 Oakley Terrace, Dennistoun, as his main address in the Post Office street directory from 1880 until he moved in his 60s to

Seafield, in Ayr, in 1901. It should be remembered that in the 1860s the University was still in the nearby High Street, less than a mile away; its move westwards was a fatal blow to Salmon's great plans.

At the bottom of Westercraigs is Annfield Place, terraced houses formerly occupied by lawyers, doctors and engineers – and now the location of the offices of the same professions, since these people don't live in Dennistoun, respectable though it is. But once off Duke Street such terraces replicate themselves and are still quality housing, with the larger villas lying just to the westward. At the top of the hill is the delightful Broompark Circus. Hereabouts it is really hard to believe that you are in Glasgow's East End. Just north of this area were the tobacco factories, and some of the land abandoned is being developed for modern quality housing. Gentrification is nibbling at the edges of Dennistoun.

Glasgow's connection with tobacco goes back to the eighteenth century and the tobacco lords, who made their wealth from the trade in the weed with the American colonies. The cigarette industry was a much later development, making the fortunes of such as Stephen Mitchell, whose legacy endowed the Mitchell Library in the city. One of his factories was located at Alexandra Parade, and is now refurbished as a collection of studios, the Wasp Factory, for arts workers. Next to it stands the Players' factory, an imposing, though rather late example of Art Deco completed in the early 1950s. This too has ceased cigarette production and was refurbished as a business centre for high-tech and advertising firms. Today Glasgow's only connection with tobacco lies sadly in the continued high consumption by its citizens of cigarettes, and the consequent high mortality rates.

Alexandra Parade is a pleasant street of solid tenements, with neat gardens on the north side and neat shops on the south, which leads to Alexandra Park. Outside is found a good example of Glasgow ironwork, a fountain beside the park gates. But if this impresses, you are in for a greater delight. Inside the park can be found another fountain, possibly the finest example of the work of the Saracen Iron Foundry still to be seen in Glasgow. Walter Macfarlane built this at Possil, and exhibited it at the 1901 Empire Exhibition; thereafter it was relocated to the park, and it has recently been restored. The classical figures represent Art, Literature, Science and Commerce.

I was taking some photographs, and got into conversation, as is often unavoidable in Glasgow. A local, obviously proud of the fountain, told me that there used to be fish in it, and that as a kid he would come and catch them.

'It's disgraceful,' he added. 'There should still be fish in it.'

'Maybe if you hadn't kept catching them, there still would be?' I suggested.

Alexandra Park was opened in 1870, supposed to be an East End equivalent of the West End's Kelvingrove, a polite watering place. The westward flight of the middle classes has left the folk of Dennistoun with a huge area for recreation, and a very fine park.

Formerly the inhabitants, and especially the weans, had more exciting attractions. Before the motorway the Monklands canal separated Dennistoun from the city to the north, and the canal banks were a favourite recreational spot, especially the waterfall at Riddrie Locks, which flowed once the locks became derelict. Further on at Riddrie Knowes were the Sugerolly Mountains, multicoloured chemical deposits where the kids would go sledging in winter, doubtless at great but unknown threats to their health.

Just after the park gates lies the former United Free Church built in 1904, and whose hall was designed by James Salmon II, grandson of the original Dennistoun planner. Salmon didn't get the contract for the church, to his chagrin, but history has turned his hall into the modern church, while the church itself has been converted into flats. A fine Faith, Hope and Love motif crowns the building. Just further on Kennyhill Square, with its prim bowling green, is the heart of Dennistoun respectability, with trim tenements and wally closes. Jack House was brought up here, and describes his boyhood in *Pavement in the Sun.*

At the far end of the Parade, where the park ends, you come to Haghill, an area built later than the Parade and of poorer tenemented housing; here you feel you are struggling to keep your feet above the waters of the East End. This feeling is confirmed as you walk south down Cumbernauld Road towards Duke Street and overlook the lands towards Parkhead, once occupied by the chemical works, but now occupied by a bakery. A pub unashamedly proclaiming its sectarian allegiance and a criminal lawyer's office announces that even douce

Dennistoun has its underbelly. I stooped to take a photo of the quaint mural in the lawyer's window. Out of the aforementioned pub staggered a punter, watching me curiously, then stating, 'He'll no get ye aff'.

I asked for an explanation and found out that my new friend thought I was in need of legal aid, in relation to some unspecified offence, and recommended another pratictioner to me.

'He gets ivverybody aff,' I was assured, and noted the fact for future use.

From Duke Street station, Duke Street, the longest in Britain, stretches away east. Staying on the Dennistoun side of the railway it is one world, but a few yards on the opposite, it is another. There are no waste plots in Dennistoun but as you head east along Duke Street towards Parkhead you enter the third world of abandoned rubbish, waste ground occupied by dookits, and boarded-up and even burnt-out housing. You can understand the desperation with which the respectable working classes sought to differentiate themselves from the underclass. To this day the sternest critics of the lumpenproletariat are the better-off working class.

Heading back along Duke Street this underworld is left behind, and we are passing again through well-maintained shops and tenements. To the north of Duke Street at Whitehill Street was the home of another famous Glasgow entertainer, Dorothy Paul, whose *Revelations of a Rejected Soprano* describes Dennistoun in the 1940s and '50s. This warm and amusing book tells of a mid-twentieth century working-class upbringing and life, with sympathy and a lack of the sentimentalism so often an aspect of Glasgow *sterrheid* writing.

Dorothy went to Whitehill School in Dennistoun, which, before comprehensive education, was the senior secondary for a large part of Glasgow's East End. It is therefore unsurprising that it was the nursery of much popular talent, especially in the fields of entertainment and culture. Dorothy admits in her autobiography that she was not a model pupil, and her irreverent attitude to her teachers probably didn't help:

> We were waiting for the teacher to arrive when who should walk in the door but Tojo the Japanese war criminal. I thought he had been hanged, but no he was a maths teacher in Whitehill Senior Secondary.

Our (history) teacher was a ringer for John Christie the mass murderer. He drooled over blood and gore, and later 'found God'. He ended going around the streets of Glasgow making a cult of himself.

Dorothy's career has had its ups and downs, and when after a difficult period she had re-established herself, she returned to Whitehill to pioneer her first one-woman show for the staff and pupils. I had been fortunate enough to teach Dorothy history when she was an outstanding mature student at Clydebank College and was also fortunate to be invited to this performance. And triply fortunate in that the comments on my teaching abilities in her book are thankfully less critical than those on her Whitehill history teacher. Aside from Dorothy, the school produced Lulu, Rikki Fulton the entertainer, Jack House the writer on Glasgow's history, as well as Adam Macnaughtan, composer of modern-day street songs, and Alasdair Gray, author of *Lanark*, and considered by many to be Scotland's greatest living writer. Quite a crop.

Dennistoun denizens have produced many autobiographies, and I have referred to some. (In fact they have produced more than any other area of the city, far ahead of Bridgeton and Gorbals, poor seconds.) Common themes emerge from perusing these. Most Dennistounians were the offspring of skilled or white-collar workers. Dorothy's dad was an electrician, Jack House's a steelworks clerk, Rikki Fulton's was a locksmith (he first worked in Singers in Clydebank but later opened his own shop). Most also appear to have had 'kirkie' upbringings; the Boys Brigade, the Church Choir and so on. Apart from the inevitable involvement in the Co-operative Society, few in Dennistoun appear to have had serious political leanings in an otherwise political city. Their lives were a far cry from the standard visions of Glasgow working-class life – or mostly they were.

Once the Carnegie Library, built in the 1890s, appears on your right just off Duke Street you are back near your starting place, with Salmon's villas and terraces on that right side, and the tenements on your left. Here in Garfield Street was where Lulu lived, but her experience of Dennistoun was not happy – or typical. A little further on lie the ruins of the corporation abbatoir where her father worked; symbolically it straddles the railway line between Dennistoun and Bridgeton. For Lulu's dad was a drunkard and a wife-beater, as she makes clear in her autobiography. Further he was a part of the East End semi-criminal underworld, regularly stealing quantities of meat from the abbatoir and selling it to local butchers.

The song *Cod Liver Oil and the Orange Juice* describes an unsavoury character at the Dennistoun Palais; he gets unseemingly drunk and then behaves badly to a young lady. The song emphasises that he was *not* from Dennistoun:

> Oot o the east there came a hard man
> Oh, ho aa the wye fae Brigton.

> Went intae a pub, came oot paralytic
> Oh, ho v.p. and cider, a helluva mixture

I feel sure that the inhabitants of Dennistoun would have looked disapprovingly at Lulu's dad, and ascribed his bad behaviour to his Bridgeton origins. And ascribed their own avoidance of such a fate to their good fortune in being raised in an area which, above all, valued and epitomised working-class respectability.

For the vast majority of working people, even in 'political' Glasgow, life was the pursuit of the calculus of differential advantage. The search was for a better job, for a better house in a better area, or betterment abroad. Apart from a minority who were politically engaged and committed, the mass of working people sought improvement – or escape, escape in entertainment, in sport as a career or as a supporter, in taking to the hills and mountains – or in engaging in a political career. Unions, the Labour Party and for a while the Co-ops offered social solidarity for working people, but also importantly, career outlets for a minority of them. These political activities, or even joining the masons or the Kirk, were forms of this incremental advantage. (In the slums and ghettoes, these aspirations were replaced by crime.) Dennistoun epitomises this search for improvement. No Mean Streets rather than No Mean City, that's Dennistoun.

Parkhead

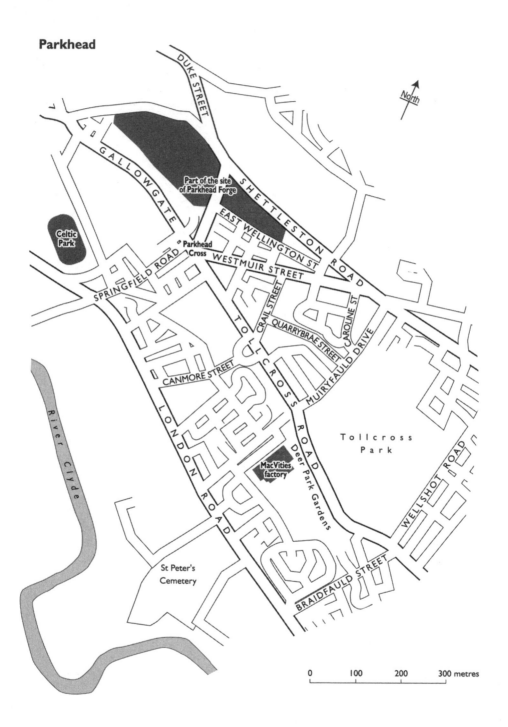

DUKE STREET

GALLOWGATE

SHETTLESTON ROAD

Part of the site
of Parkhead Forge

Celtic
Park

EAST WELLINGTON ST

Parkhead
Cross

WESTMUIR STREET

SPRINGFIELD ROAD

CRAIL STREET

QUARRYBRAE STREET

CAROLINE ST

MUIRYFAULD DRIVE

CANMORE STREET

TOLLCROSS ROAD

Tollcross
Park

LONDON ROAD

Deer Park Gardens

WELLSHOT ROAD

MacVities
factory

River Clyde

St Peter's
Cemetery

BRAIDFAULD STREET

North

| 0 | 100 | 200 | 300 metres |

CHAPTER THIRTEEN

Parkhead: Paradise Lost

TO SOME THE NAME may conjure up Paradise, though in truth the Parkhead district does not really start until one has gone to the east side of the stadium of Celtic FC. The west side lies in Bridgeton. Parkhead has the same rich heavy industrial past as its westerly neighbour, but without Bridgeton's manifold pre-industrial references, and possibly with a more problematic future.

The first known mention of Parkhead dates from 1794 when there was an inn of that name at the junction of the Tollcross Road and the Gallowgate. Six years after there was a post office at Parkhead, and round about were opened a series of coal mines and engineering works. With the surrounding weavers' settlements, the population of the area was still only around 2,000. A century later, Parkhead and its satellites including Tollcross had a population of 80,000, a growth down to the development of the iron and steel industry and in particular to Parkhead Forge. David Willox wrote his *Memoirs of Parkhead* in the 1920s, describing the district from the 1850s onwards, when it was still a collection of industrial villages in a semi-rural setting. The tenements appeared from the 1880s. Parkhead, with its neighbours of Tollcross and Shettleston, still retains examples of the pre-tenement style of cottage housing, largely disappeared elsewhere from Glasgow's streets. Whitelaw's pub in Tollcross Road near Parkhead Cross, for example, retains the look of a pre-industrial weaver's cottage, though much remodelled.

The focus of the community was and is the present Cross of Parkhead. Its original name was the Sheddens, from an Anglo-Saxon word meaning 'the parting of the ways'. Some older people still know it by this name, which is very appropriate, since the junction is in the form of a K, rather than a proper Cross. The buildings around Parkhead Cross reflect its glory days. The Glasgow Savings Bank, designed by architect John Keppie, is the finest building in Parkhead, with its embossed lettering and sculpted figures. The solid sandstone tenements at the guschets of the ᴋ-junction tell of when this was a vibrant, growing and prosperous community, as do JR Rhind's Carnegie Library and the Co-operative building, in the adjacent Tollcross Road and Westmuir Street respectively. But a walk a short distance in any direction from the Kross shows that these glory days, and most of the buildings, workplaces and people associated with them, are long gone. Paradise Lost here.

The stadium remains, however, despite past plans to move to an outer-city site. Celtic came here in 1888, after being founded by Brother Walfrid. The ostensible aim of the club was to help the poor and needy, and doubtless it did. But the creation of Celtic ꜰᴄ also was an expression of the desire of the Catholic clergy to keep their faithful from supporting other teams where they might mix with the unfaithful. To this day the Catholic clergy have free entry to Paradise – or at least to Celtic Park. Of great influence there, their influence on the Labour movement was disproportionate and negative. A study of Scottish Labour leaders in the twentieth century showed that over 50% were secularists or atheists. Of the remaining religiously-inclined half, only 14% were Catholics, roughly their representation in the population at large. Yet because in key areas the clergy could have a large influence on how working-class Catholics voted, and these votes could turn otherwise finely balanced elections, Catholic views became difficult to challenge. The Red Clydesiders for example stayed silent on segregated schooling and on birth-control issues; even Maxton, to his discredit, even he.

Duke Street, Britain's longest street, starts in central Glasgow and ends at Parkhead Cross. It still leads to Parkhead Forge. Not to the steel foundry, but to the present shopping centre which took over the name of the industrial undertaking. This has brought welcome jobs to the East End, of the kind that the residual, unskilled population can perform. Though much of the work is part-time and casual, the new Forge employs almost as many people as the old one did in its peace-time glory. Most of the work is unskilled, and much of it is low paid. People welcome the jobs, though many of the local shops have been killed off, and the banks and similar facilities have moved into The Forge. It is also good to see a brown site used for such a development rather than another out-of-town blight being built at some motorway interchange. When you look at this shopping complex, you realise how vast Parkhead Forge was, for much of the space left by its final closure in 1981 is still awaiting development. Apart from its huge wall, the only part of the original forge left is the main office building in Shettleston Road, now housing an ironically named New Life Church amidst the surrounding dereliction.

The forge at Parkhead was founded in 1837 by the Reoch brothers, beginning modestly like many others at that time, forging iron from scrap. It was taken over by David Napier who expanded it to produce steel for the growing shipbuilding industry and was then sold to a partnership including the first William Beardmore in 1863. Already Parkhead's biggest employer with 700 workers, Beardmore expanded the forge still further, installing the world's biggest lathe to turn propellor shafts for shipbuilding. When William Beardmore Junior took over in 1879 he replaced the 100-ton steam hammer *Samson* with the 500-ton *Goliath*, again the biggest in the world in its time. He also installed the more efficient Siemens open-hearth furnaces at the plant, which were probably the most advanced of their kind in the world around 1900.

Parkhead Forge produced not only steel forgings for ships, but also for construction work, and supplied William Arrol of Bridgeton with 20,000 tons of cast steel for the building of Tower Bridge in London. Covering 18 hectares, the works employed 5,000 men in their peacetime days before 1914, but even then much of their work was for the expanding arms race. In 1905 Beardmore's built the 110-feet-high gun-quenching tower for casting artillery, atop the existing building. At the time, this made Parkhead Forge the highest building in Scotland, and it was dubbed 'Parkhead Cathedral'. The tower was demolished in 1969 as the works contracted.

Beardmore's dominated life in Parkhead. Almost every family had someone who worked in the Forge, and the firm owned many other ancillary works nearby, such as the crane works and the wheel and axle works, both in Rigby Street – as well as a commercial motor factory in the appropriately named Van Street. Nor was this all; Beardmore bought an entire steelworks at Mossend to ensure quality in his steel supplies, and also laid out a new shipyard in Dalmuir to build ships himself. Before WW1 he was Scotland's largest employer, and the firms directly or partly controlled by him employed almost 100,000 workers.

The furnaces of the forge burned night and day, brightening the Parkhead sky, and the reverberation of the hammers created a constant noise. Tom Bell, an early Parkhead socialist, recalled in his *Pioneering Days* that in the 1880s 'the smell of oil and smoke, the thud of the *Samson* hammer and the glare of the furnaces were fast banishing the sights and sounds and colours of the country'.

Another Beardmore socialist, Davie Kirkwood remembered that when the *Goliath* hammer was installed and in operation, 'the whole district quivered as in an earthquake'.

William Beardmore was nothing if not ambitious. He helped finance some of Shackleton's polar explorations, and had the Beardmore Glacier named after him (Shackleton repaid Beardmore by having an affair with his wife). But he overreached and was verging on bankruptcy when he was forced to amalgamate with Vickers in 1902 and make the company a limited one, ending total family control. The First World War gave him a breathing space. Parkhead employed 20,000 people working 24 hours a day producing munitions. Beardmore was nicknamed the Field Marshall of Industry, and knighted as Lord Invernairn.

After the war, at a time of depression he tried to expand into new areas like aircraft building and motor-car production, but the firm was effectively bankrupt and the banks took over in the mid-1920s, forcing Sir William into an early retirement. He died in 1936, before which many of his schemes had crashed and much of his empire had been dismantled. The forge carried on, boosted again by war in 1939 and reconstruction afterwards, but on an ever-reducing scale as shipbuilding contracted.

On Parkhead Forge were centred many of the events of the period of Red Clydeside a century ago. Davie Kirkwood was convenor of shop stewards at Beardmore's and wrote his account of those times in his *My Life of Revolt*. The fact that this had a preface by Winston Churchill showed that Kirkwood mellowed with time. Elected to Parliament in 1922 for the ILP he eventually moved to Labour. He was knighted, spending his comfortable retirement in Bearsden, far from Parkhead, with the odd trip to the House of Lords.

Kirkwood was criticised by many for his cosy relationship with Beardmore, and during the Dilution Crisis of 1915 he broke the struggle of the Clyde Workers' Committee by doing a separate deal at Parkhead Forge to introduce dilution and boost war production, in return for concessions to the unions. John Maclean attacked Kirkwood and others of the CWC for not opposing the war, but simply using it as a means to get improvements from the employers on trades union issues. Maclean's criticism was apposite, but unfortunately the likes of Kirkwood probably represented more accurately the aspirations of the trades union members. There is a road that leads to the House of Lords, and one to a pauper's grave; Kirkwood took the former, and John Maclean the latter.

And there is a road to Shettleston, called, unsurprisingly, Shettleston Road. Walking along this street gives you an idea of the scale of the old forge. John Cairney, the actor, was born in Parkhead and he recalls, in his *East End to West End,* a trip along Shettleston Road which broadened his horizons. Parkhead kids used to jump onto lorries to hitch lifts in the 1930s, and hop off at traffic lights. But one driver became so annoyed at this practice that he drove through all the red lights till he got out of Glasgow. When the lorry stopped a terrified Cairney was deposited on the pavement:

> But as I looked up I saw a castle and I was absolutely stunned. What a sight it was: Edinburgh Castle. It was a fantastic wonderland to a Glasgow keelie.

Westmuir Street is a pleasant street to amble along, and on the right is the Eastern Co-op Building of 1903, which in turn has a plaque commemorating the Parkhead and Westmuir Economical Society of 1831, the area's first co-op. On the left is Parkhead School, built in 1878, but now in disrepair and largely disused. A cut along Crail Street takes you to Quarrybrae Street and an interesting building. This looks like a school, and though it functioned as a further education college annex for a while, it was actually built a century ago as a Model Lodging House for the multitudes of unskilled workers who flocked here to work. A building workers' strike in Parkhead was broken at that time by bringing in Irish labour to complete the work. Many strikebreakers stayed at the Model and old Parkhead folk used to call this Scabby Loan in remembrance. At present it is being converted to residential accommodation, but this far from the city centre one imagines it will not be a yuppie zone.

Few Glasgow working-class areas do not have enclaves of superior dwellings; in the days when people had to live close to their work, housing for clerical and professional workers within distance of employment was necessary. The greatest surprise in this area is the trio of streets bordering Tollcross Park – just up Quarrybrae from the old Model, too. Muirfauld Drive is a terrace of solid semi-detached villas, overlooking the park, and Tennyson Drive and Dunnover Drive are scarcely less fine. But drop downhill to Caroline Street and those roads around it and you are in one of the worst ghettoes in the city: interwar housing, much abandoned and even burned out, festooned with rubbish and the graffiti of despair. Other ghettoes abound between the main thoroughfares of Parkhead, for example around Macbeth and Canmore Street; many are in the three-storey tenements that were built by the council in the '20s and '30s.

But poor old Glasgow Council doesn't get everything wrong. Tollcross Park is a Glasgow success story, and its restoration a wonderful boon to the people of Parkhead and other areas adjoining it. The lands here were owned by the Dunlop family. The Dunlops had been amongst the city's leading tobacco lords, but moved out of that trade and into the coming thing; coal and iron. They sank many coal pits in Tollcross, but they wanted the fuel mainly to smelt iron, and in the early 1800s established the Clyde Iron Works at Tollcross. They were lucky enough to allow a Shettleston man, John Nielson, to try his newfangled hot blast in their furnaces, allowing a great reduction in fuel costs and improvement of the quality of iron. The family prospered as never before, and Colin Dunlop became Glasgow's first post-Reform Act MP in 1835. The family mansion was built in the grounds of Tollcross by James Bryce in the 1840s, in Scots Baronial style. The Dunlops suffered in the depression of the 1870s, with falling iron prices and the emergence of trades unionism in their workforce, and a series of strikes followed as they tried to cut wages. Steel, not iron, was now the new idea, and by the 1890s the Dunlops were bankrupt, selling the park to Glasgow Council for £30,000 (about £3 million today).

The mansion became a children's museum, then became derelict, as too did the Winter Gardens. Lottery money restored the latter in 1996, and locals successfully blocked plans to sell the mansion as luxury flats. Instead it was converted to sheltered housing for local people in 1993. The park has designated walks and a children's farm within its boundaries, and is excellently maintained and well used. Also, a new swimming pool has been built in a former area of the park, of Olympic standard. On the south side of the park is probably the finest set of tenements in the whole East End, on a section of Tollcross Road known as Deer Park Gardens, giving a marvellous architectural line up the brae towards Parkhead proper. Behind it is the McVities biscuit factory, still employing about 600 people and probably the largest of the few industrial units left in Parkhead.

Parkhead is one of the few areas of Glasgow without a railway. Parkhead Station was closed in 1962. It used to be well served by trams, however, and the last one in 1962 ran to the famous satellite of Parkhead known as Auchenshuggle. This event produced its usual Glasgow ditty, a variation on the *Last Train to San Fernando* lyric:

Last Tram tae Auchenshuggle, Last Tram tae Auchenshuggle
If you miss this one you'll never get another one
Biddy biddy bum bum tae Auchenshuggle

Auchenshuggle is no joke, but another poverty-stricken ghetto of degraded housing and poor facilities on either side of Braidfauld Street. The shops here, such as Honest Joe's which advertises 'Tic for the needy', are a mocking counterpoint to the gloss of the new Forge. At Potter Street off the London Road were found the Govancroft Potteries, another Glasgow pottery whose wares are now collectible – since it closed in the late 1980s. Amidst all this urban decay a sylvan interlude is called for. On the opposite side of London Road to Potter Street is St Peter's cemetery, and a lane leads past the cemetary. Take the lane, braving the rubbish, and you come to the banks of the Clyde at one of its most delightful spots, which seems a million miles away from Auchenshuggle.

Here the river takes a series of vast loops between the city and Rutherglen and Cambuslang on the opposite bank. Even when this area was dominated by heavy industry, much of it was undeveloped. In the 1930s James Cowan, in *From Glasgow's Treasure Chest*, recorded the wonder he felt when he saw 'in a wide flat valley more than forty horses grazing … and fields of cabbage, corn and potatoes filling up most of the land enclosed by the river'. Now much of the industrial waste has been grown over and the site abounds with flora and fauna of every description. Westwards takes you back to Glasgow Green, eastwards to Carmyle and – eventually – Lanark on a walk/cycleway stretching 35 miles. The original idea of Oor City Faithers was not a cycle track and walkway here, but instead to cover the area with an extension of the motorway system, and to put all the bends of the Clyde into an underground pipe. I didn't make that up, honest. Work on the revised M74 extension has now begun in this area, but takes a different route into the city, south of the River Clyde.

As well as the delights of the river, here by the Clyde's banks you will find a strange wall that crosses the path. Till the end of the nineteenth century this was known as Harvie's Dyke, and its tale is worth telling. Around 1800 Parkhead was a collection of mining and weaving hamlets, whose inhabitants regularly fought each other as a form of entertainment. However, faced with a common danger they could unite, and the colliers, weavers and others of Parkhead joined with those of Carmyle and Dalmarnock in defence of their traditional rights of access to the Clyde. In 1819 Thomas Harvie, a local distiller, acquired the lands of Westhorn and built a dyke at both ends of his property right down into the river to prevent pedestrian access to the banks. In July 1822 a large mob demolished the dyke with picks and crowbars. The Enniskillen Dragoons were called out, shots fired, and the leaders of the protest arrested and imprisoned. A fund was raised for their defence, the case went to the House of Lords, Harvie was defeated and the men released. Harvie disappeared to Ireland after some shady financial dealings, but so too did the £384 surplus of the fund raised for the men's defence. A medal was struck to commemorate the deed in 1829.

This was just one aspect of the radicalism of Parkhead. In 1820 many of the weavers and colliers had struck in the fight for parliamentary reform, in the so-called Radical War. It is argued by some that the address calling for strike action and reform was actually drawn up in Parkhead itself. The area was also a stronghold of Chartism in the 1840s. Some of the first Co-operatives were founded in Parkhead, the earliest being the Parkhead and Westmuir Economical Society in 1831. In 1839 a Scientific Association was opened with a library of almost 1,000 books, sustained by local working men. The militancy around the time of the First World War had solid roots in Parkhead's past.

Negotiating your way along the river behind the former Belvidere Hospital you re-emerge into post-industrial Parkhead at the junction of London Road and Springfield Road. In the old days it was the Forge's quenching tower that was visible from everywhere in Parkhead; now it is the cantilevers of Celtic Park. Springfield Road used to be known as Dry Thrapple Lane, from the stour raised before it was paved and before Glasgow people lost much of their Scots dialect. Old photographs of its neat tenements and tidy shops only emphasise the state of the street today, though it improves a bit towards the Cross, where we are returning.

In the old days if your thrapple was dry you no doubt repaired to the Black Bull Inn in the Gallowgate just west of Parkhead Cross. This building dated from 1760 and was reputed to be the oldest in the whole area. It is commemorated in a poem by John Breckenridge, celebrating the opening of a baker's establishment near to the pub:

It's auld Ne'er day an! We're met i' the 'Bull'
Wi oor hearts dancin' licht, an' a bowl flowing full
Let envy and spite throw aff a' disguise
And drink to young Gibbie that's gi'en us the pies.

A pie and a pint have a long pedigree in Parkhead. There is still a Black Bull here, but not the original one as the current pub is situated in a tenement built in 1902.

The owner of the Black Bull also produced his own light beverages, but was bought out by a Falkirk man, JK Barr, in the 1880s. Barr's successors in the family produced a drink called Iron-Brew in 1901, which probably found an appreciative marked in thirsty forge workers. The firm, and Irn-Bru as it is now called, has gone from strength to strength, surviving the 1930s depression and the now-globalised market. The drink outsells Coca-Cola in Scotland and Barr themselves have been going global, becoming especially popular in Russia, which shares Scotland's sweet tooth. Barr employs 1,200, but moved its manufacturing capacity to Cumbernauld some years ago. As this book went to press it was announced that the Parkhead headquarters of Barr would also close.

Parkhead is probably just too far from the centre and West End of Glasgow to share much in its reinvention as a city of culture, city of finance, city of lifestyle. Whatever one's thoughts on the Forge shopping centre, it has possibly saved Parkhead from the kind of decline seen in certain other areas of the city, for example in Possil. Parkhead (with its satellites) is now an area with a low-tech, low-skilled population, much declined from its height of 75,000 to about 25,000. It is hard to imagine the prosperity and skills base of a century ago returning to the area in any foreseeable future. Indeed, it is more likely that a European trophy might return to Paradise.

Rutherglen

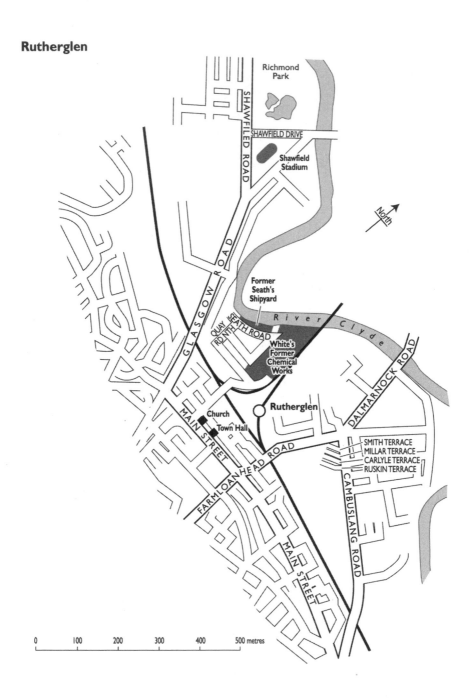

Richmond Park

SHAWFIELD DRIVE

Shawfield Stadium

SHAWFIELD ROAD

North

GLASGOW ROAD

Former Seath's Shipyard

River Clyde

QUAY RD SEATH ROAD
RD NTH

White's Former Chemical Works

DALMARNOCK ROAD

Rutherglen

Church

Town Hall

MAIN STREET

FARMLOAN HEAD ROAD

SMITH TERRACE
MILLAR TERRACE
CARLYLE TERRACE
RUSKIN TERRACE

CAMBUSLANG ROAD

MAIN STREET

0   100   200   300   400   500 metres

CHAPTER FOURTEEN

Rutherglen Regained

'RU'GLEN'S WEE ROON reid lums reekin' briskly' do not do so within Glasgow City's boundaries. This despite the fact that the closest point in Rutherglen to George Square is less than a mile and a half as the crow flies. By contrast you are still more than ten miles from Edinburgh on the M8 when a sign announces you are in that city. Glasgow's absurdly constricted boundaries are nowhere more apparent than with the case of Rutherglen. Insult is added to injury when it is recalled that historically Ru'glen was one of the Glasgow Burghs which sent an MP to Parliament before 1832. A previous local government reorganisation had given the burgh to Glasgow, only for it to be snatched back again in the mid 1990s – and given to *South* Lanarkshire, of which county it is one of the most northerly parts.

Rutherglen is Glasgow's lost territory, its *terra irridenta*, which in every way – economically, transportwise and culturally – is part of Glasgow. I am slightly less enthusiasic about Ru'glen's neighbour, Cambuslang. Here there is more of a feel of Lanarkshire. During the Civil Rights struggles of the 1960s, HL Mencken said that one day in the far distant future Mississippi might attain the level of social progress reached by Poland between the World Wars. I have no such utopian hopes for Lanarkshire. But Ru'glen now, that's a fine wee toon. The civic motto of the town was *Ex fumo fama*, which basically means 'Let the lums reek'.

Rutherglen is possibly older than Glasgow, with a good claim to be Scotland's first Royal burgh, its charter dating from David I in 1126. In The Middle Ages Rutherglen was the head of River Clyde navigation and more commercially important than Glasgow. Around 1330 the town paid 5% of all Scotland's burgh taxes. It was a significant ecclesiastical centre and had a fine Norman church. In this kirk Wallace made a truce with the English in 1297, and here too Sir John Menteith later treated with the English to betray Wallace at Robroyston. Rutherglen Castle was strategically important and was captured by Robert the Bruce in 1305, and later demolished after the defeat of Mary Queen of Scots at the Battle of Langside. According to the *New Statistical Account* this castle had an inscription dating from 1325 which must have been one of the earliest such in Scots. It is delightful and deserves an airing here:

> He that sittis doun to ye henv[?] for to eite
> Forgetting to gyf god thankis for his meite
> Syne rysis upe and his grace oure pass
> Sittis doun lyk ane oxe and rysis lyk ane ass

With the growth of Glasgow, Rutherglen's importance declined, though in 1679 it was the scene of stirring historical events. A group of Covenanters rode into the town and at the Mercat Cross burnt various documents associated with Charles II and Episcopacy. And in the Declaration of Rutherglen these early republicans declared the king overthrown. The insurgents had their success over Bloody Clavers (Bonnie Dundee) at the battle of Drumclog soon after. However, the Covenanters met their nemesis at Bothwell Brig later in the same year. These events form the backbone of Scott's novel, *Old Mortality*. Ru'glens stagnation and decline was arrested and turned round by the industrialisation of the West of Scotland.

In his *History of Rutherglen and East Kilbride* (1793), David Ure gave the number of its inhabitants as 1630, adding 'The population, owing to the growth of manufactures, is on the increase'. Ru'glen was still mainly a weaving town, with 250 weavers and just 60 colliers, according to Ure. The discovery of large coal deposits in the area led to the sinking of mines and an account from the early nineteenth century stated that now Rutherglen 'was chiefly inhabited by coal hewers.' One of the mines, the Farme Colliery, built its own steam engine to drain the mine in 1810. It operated there till 1915, and is now in the Summerlee Industrial Museum in Coatbridge. Farmeloan Road and Farme Cross still today commemorate this pit. The Stonelaw mine was another. Soon the mines were followed by bleach-fields and dyeworks, characteristic of the early, textile phase of industrialisation, and then heavy industry arrived in turn.

In 1808 the Whites opened their Shawfield Chemical Works in Rutherglen. If you arrive from Glasgow by train at Rutherglen station, the site of the works is the large area to your right, now a rickle of buildings forming a trading and industrial estate. Shawfield closed in 1965 after a century and a half of infamy. The Whites ran the works here, and others in their empire, as a family company for over a century. The third White, John, was a Christian philanthropist, a Free Kirker after the Disruption of 1843. This fine man gave generously to missions to Christianise the African heathen, and to the building of the Christian Institute in Glasgow's Bothwell Street. This fine man was a financial backer of the alcohol prohibition campaign, and also of the Glasgow Liberal Party, paying off the debts of the Liberal Club. This fine man, who conducted extensive family prayers every day, was given a peerage by Gladstone, and became Lord Overtoun, buying a 3,000-acre estate at Bowling on the Clyde. This fine man was a mass murderer. If there were a God, White would be in Hell.

The Shawfield works produced chrome, indeed they were the largest producer in Britain, possibly the largest in the world. At first chrome was used in the dyestuffs industry, but later the development of electro-plating created an insatiable demand for the metal. The production of this commodity made the Shaws into millionaires, yet their legacy continues to kill and maim. The effluent of the works ran into the Mall's Mire burn and then into the Clyde, untreated. Even today the level of chromium in the burn is 825 times the permitted amount. Chromium is highly carcinogenic. With 1% of Scotland's population, Rutherglen and its neighbour Cambuslang have 25% of all Scotland's children's leukaemia cancers. Today, not a century ago. These towns also suffer a high concentration of otherwise rare children's kidney tumors.

During their lifetime it has been estimated that the Shawfield works dumped 275 million litres a year of toxic phenols and cyanides into the surrounding water table. The air the factory produced was virtually unbreathable. As well of having high incidence of cancers such as those of the nose and throat, White's workers suffered severe respiratory problems from fumes laced with cyanide. Locals called the men 'White's Canaries' after their skin colour, or simply 'White's Dead Men'. One historian writes that 'The works were a filthy place where men laboured for 12 hours a day under degrading and dangerous conditions at mimimal wages'. These wages were four (old) pence an hour for labourers.

White would stand at the gates of the factory at the end of shifts and chastise workers leaving if they had flecks of chrome on their clothing or footwear, shouting, 'Hey, man, gang back and daud yer shin. Div ye no see y're cairrying awa siller when ye cairry crum on yet bitts.' The work in this Inferno was largely unskilled, and the labourers difficult to organise, but they took part in the upsurge of strikes known as the New Unionism, embracing the unskilled and semi-skilled workers, in the 1880s and 1890s. Just at the peak of his self-satisfied fame, when he had been knighted and was preparing the launch of a Christian Revivalist Crusade, White's Dead Men walked. Walked out of the factory in 1899 demanding a union and the right to be treated as human beings. The strike became a national issue, largely because the workers' case was taken up by Keir Hardie.

Hardie wrote detailed articles in the *Labour Leader*, the newspaper of the Independent Labour Party, which exposed the conditions under which White exploited his men. These texts were made into a pamphlet, *White's Slaves: Lord Overtoun, Chrome Charities and Cant,* and helped publicise their strike. But possibly the men relied too much on Hardie, and he soon had other fish to fry. With the formation of the Labour Party (LRC) in 1900, Hardie ceased to give White's his close attention. The men were forced back to work, having won minor concessions. The press and the middle-class political and church organisations of the day stood behind White, and his obituaries in newspapers in 1908 were sickening odes to his Christian integrity. An extracted example:

A Christian of a noble type
A man of God from youth
A benefactor of the race
A champion of the truth.

A Christian Sabbatarian, White campaigned against the opening of the Glasgow People's Palace on a Sunday, the working men's only day off. Yet he ran his works seven days a week, and sacked workers who failed to work Sundays. Only the *Glasgow Herald* mentioned the 'Overtoun Exposure' in its obituary, the rest of the press ignored it.

And still, a century later, the Ru'glen weans die.

Not all the pollution around Rutherglen was due to White's, though a 1990s estimate put the cost at cleaning up the Shawfield works alone at £20 million. These works are just one of the 27 dangerous sites in and around the town, possibly the highest concentration in the UK. One of these was the ground of Glencairn Park FC, where the terraces were built from industrial waste, and were 26 times over the allowable limits for various pollutants. Another major polluter was the Clydebridge Steel works, opened in the 1880s in the river bend north of Rutherglen. This huge mill operated for more than a century before it was run down in the 1980s. There are still large polluted sites hereabouts, simply capped by a covering of earth. Others, similarly untreated, have been built over by housing and shops.

Anyway, let's cheer ourselves up and go walkabout. There may no longer be wee roon reid lums reekin in Ru'glen, but there is lots to see. From Rutherglen station take the exit to Farmeloan Road, and walk south to Farme Cross. Here is the old industrial centre of Rutherglen, which was replaced by trading and commercial estates built on the capped poisoned lands. While this capping stopped airborne dust pollution it did nothing to stop the chemicals leeching into the water table. And most of these sites set up in the 1970s, bringing light industry to the town, are now themselves derelict and abandoned. Not exactly where you would expect to find a Conservation Area, but there is one.

A small cluster of streets with the names of famous writers lies here. The Terraces of Smith, Millar, Carlyle and Ruskin commemorate eminent Scottish men of letters of the eighteenth and nineteenth centuries. These are fine cottage-style rows of houses, with small front and back gardens, recently restored and given protected status. A local resident playing fitba' with his son told me they had originally been miners' rows; if so they were far superior to the average of the sort. I told him I was annexing Ru'glen to Glasgow and asked his opinion.

'I dinnae mind. I'm fae the Gorbals.' And he pointed out the not-faraway high Hutchesontown flats he had moved out of. 'And it might be a good idea. Sooth Lanarkshire's a wee bit slow getting things daen,' he added. Walking back up Farmeloan Road brings you to Main Street.

Rutherglen was long a market town, having weekly markets as well as regular horse fairs, and this accounts for the width of the street, and the breadth of the pavements, which were built for stalls. With the declining use of pit ponies and of horses on the land, the last fairs were held in 1900, I had read. However, the pavements of Main Street were busy with a farmer's market the last time I arrived, offering the local inhabitants the best of country produce, and maintaining the old Ru'glen traditions. Looking along the street gives a pleasant view, especially on the north side. Dominating all is the Town Hall, with its top heavy tower, a prominent landmark from many surrounding vantage points. This was built in 1861 by Charles Wilson, and was the centre of burgh government till the mid-1970s. It is an attractive Scots Baronial revival building, and one of its features is the large collection of cast-iron lions' heads on its western wall.

I had been to the local library and seen an exhibition where South Lanarkshire had promised to return the hall to the people of Rutherglen 'by the year 2003'. The plans spoke of an arts centre, a café and various other facilities which would doubtless benefit the burgh. But as I passed, in 2004, I noticed that the work was still ongoing and far from complete. My Gorbals-born adoptive Ru'glonian was obvious correct about the slowness of the South Lanarkshire Council. If they'd been in Glasgow, it could have been done in 1999 for the Year of Architecture.

Just next to the town hall is Rutherglen's old parish church, set on a pre-Christian site; the original church dates from the late twelfth century. The leafy graveyard is a delightful spot, almost like a country kirk, with its trees and fine collection of gravestones. The entrance arch to the kirkyard dates from the 1660s, and just inside are two sentry boxes from the eighteenth century where the elders collected the offerings of the communicants. The present church was built in 1901, designed by JJ Burnet, and replaced the one built in the 1790s, which itself replaced the medieval foundation. Standing free in the kirkyard is a fine belltower, whose bell was forged in Holland in the seventeenth century. The tower is not 'Norman', as stated by some observers. Though it has a northern French look about it, the tower was constructed in the later 15th century. It had no connection with the church into which it was built, and the gable of the demolished medieval kirk can still be seen on the western side of the tower.

Just past the kirk are the offices of the *Rutherglen Reformer*, the local paper, started in 1874 and still going strong on local loyalty. Rutherglen grew from about 2,000 people in 1800 to about 30,000 in 1900, and the population has remained remarkably stable since, at around this figure. No longer here though is the Saracen Fountain which was removed in 1900 to help traffic flow, and relocated in Overtoun Park to the south. The broad pavements of Ru'glen would seem wide enough to me to take the fountain, and its reinstatement here would add much to the look of Main Street. Turning south up Mill Street takes you to the park, which was a gift to the burgh in the will of White when he died in 1908. Overtoun Park lies in middle-class Rutherglen, with its terraces and villas. A pleasant area, though with no significant buildings. But there is another possible walk from Main Street, slightly more on the wild side.

The Glasgow Road turns north towards the city, and taking it as far as and across the railway bridge brings you to the site of the former Shawfield Works. Like much of the burgh's industrial past, this has been concreted over for a trading estate, which looks even more dilapidated that the one at Farmeloan Road. Building after building is abandoned, burnt out, or partially occupied by an assortment of activities one would not like to investigate too closely. My aim was to get to Seath Street, where Ru'glen's most surprising industry had been located. Masted ships were cut off from Rutherglen when the Glasgow burghers bridged the river. But the canny Ru'glonians developed a shipbuilding industry in the 1850s, building craft that could sail under the Clyde bridges; craft like the Cluthas, which were small cargo ships, or small paddle craft for pleasure uses. Of these the *Lucy Ashton* used in England's Lake District was probably the most famous. The surprising place where this happened was Seath's yard, and it survived until after World War One. I had seen the piles and quays of the yard from the Bridgeton side of the Clyde and set off to locate them.

Many dodgy dens of dereliction later I found the yard, or at least part of it that now hosts the local boat club. Here fanatics repair their

Swann's *Views of Glasgow*, plate 3. *Glasgow from Arn's Well*
Glasgow Green in the days when it was a fashionable resort – and also a bleachfield.
Glasgow City Council (Mitchell Library)

craft, and launch them into the Clyde for trips down the river, through the weir at Glasgow Green, and onto the wide ocean. There was a great debate amongst the *cognoscenti* as to whether this was Seath's, or whether Ru'glen quay where it was located was a little up river. But for the sake of historical continuity I am prepared to accept the present boat yard as the site. Getting to the other would have involved climbing fences, dodging dogs and security guards, or even greater possible dangers.

From the Clyde, it is either back to the station, or along the Glasgow Road to verify the closeness of Glasgow and its Green to Ru'glen. Glasgow Road hereabouts is an avenue of footballing dreams. Glencairn FC's ground is on the left. The high level of poison in its construction materials didn't stop the 'Chookie Hens', as they were nicknamed, winning the Scottish Junior Cup four times. And further on is the former Shawfield stadium of Clyde FC. The 'Bully Wee', as they were called, were founded in Rutherglen in 1898, and were twice Scottish Cup winners. The absurdity of Ru'glen's exclusion from Glasgow is shown by the fact that you can shoot in Ru'glen and score in Glasgow, since part of the pitch falls within the city. Or could shoot. Clyde moved out of Rutherglen some time ago, though the stadium continues to host dog racing.

Remodelled in the 1930s as an Art Deco stadium, Shawfield was Scotland's Highbury. But to see it now, this is hard to believe. Most of the Art Deco features have gone, to be replaced by corrugated iron, or have simply decayed like the once smart entrance. I was lucky enough to see Aberdeen play a couple of times at Shawfield in the late '70s and early '80s, when some of the stadium's faded glories were still in place. But already the Clyde support was down to a thousand or so, and the grass on the pitch needed cutting. Or maybe that was a tactic to help the Bully Wee. Anyway, the Dons won.

Even before you cross the bridge from Shawfield to Glasgow Green – five minutes to the Green and 20 to George Square – you are in Glasgow. And so too should Ru'glen be. But there is another thing that needs changing. White is the only Ru'glonian to have a statue in Glasgow, in Cathedral Square. If Ru'glen ever comes back, that should go.

Bridgeton

Glasgow
Cross

HIGH STREET

SALTMARKET

St ANDREWS
SQUARE

St Andrews
Church

GREENDYKE ST

MONTEITH ROW

LONDON ROAD

BARRACK ST

GALLOWGATE

Site of
former
Abbatoir

BELGROVE ST

Bellgrove

People's
Palace
Museum

GLASGOW GREEN

KINGS DRIVE

River Clyde

ABERCROMBY STREET

Former
Templeton's
Carpet
Factory

Calton Old
Cemetery

JAMES STREET

Bridgeton
Cross

Bridgeton

LANDRESSY ST

MAIN STREET

BURNS

DALMARNOCK ROAD

FIELDEN STREET

GALLOWGATE

POPLIN
STREET

LONDON ROAD

William Arrol's
Dalmarnock Works

Dalmarnock

Former
Carstairs St Mill
of Glasgow
Cotton Company

SPRINGFIELD ROAD

North

0   100   200   300 metres

CHAPTER FIFTEEN

Around Bridgeton Cross

I COULD WELL BE in a small minority, but if I were condemned to spend eternity wandering around one part of Mungo's City, then it would be within a circle prescribed by a radius of a mile or so from Brigton Cross – or 'Bridgeton' as it is increasingly but inaccurately pronounced. Where else would you find a Venetian palace, a Byzantine mausoleum and the Shipka Pass? In the Balkan peninsula certainly, but if you didn't want to go so far from home you could just take a wee daunder instead around Bridgeton Cross in Glasgow's East End.

The territories hereabouts might seem at first infertile regions in which to seek the pleasures of urban walking. Certainly this is an area which has had a decidedly bad press, exceeded only possibly by that of the Gorbals. Those who know Glasgow from 'No Mean City'-type hearsay will associate Bridgeton with razor gangs, Billy Boy sectarianism, and some of the worst housing in Europe. James Leslie Mitchell (aka Lewis Grassic Gibbon) stated in the 1930s in *The Scottish Scene* that hereabouts were 'over a hundred and fifty thousand human beings living in such conditions as the most bitterly pressed primitive in Tierra del Feugo never envisaged'. An exaggeration certainly, but containing a deal of truth, at a time when certain areas in Glasgow shared the population density of Calcutta. But I suspect that Mitchell/Gibbon, like many others, actually wrote about Bridgeton without even having been there.

One thing that would astonish Gibbon is that today the population of Glasgow's East End area is probably a quarter of the number he quoted. Several parliamentary constituencies – including Bridgeton itself, which was the Red Clydesider and Independent Labour Party rebel James Maxton's seat – have disappeared. If John Knox were to re-inhabit his Edinburgh house today, he would recognise the Royal Mile easily after 500 years. But from the eyes in the back of his head (which he surely possesses) on his statue in the Glasgow Necropolis overlooking the greater Bridgeton district, Knox would scarcely recognise the place after only 50 years.

If one looks at John Hume's *Industrial Archeology of Glasgow*, Bridgeton was home to so many factories that you wonder where the people were. Bridgeton at its height was even more industrial than Govan or Anderston, which possibly made it the most industrialised few square miles on the planet. Nowhere have the effects of Glasgow's industrial decline been as visible as here. Indeed, here started the ill-fated Glasgow East Area Renewal (GEAR) project in the 1970s, where huge areas of substandard housing were cleared and attempts were made to attract new manufacturing industry to the area, to replace the large works which had closed down or were in decline. But the industrial closures continued. These included the Arrol Bridge and Crane Works in the mid-1980s, and Anderson Strathclyde Mining Machinery (formerly Mavor and Coulson), which folded with the closure of the mines in 1992. Many more proud names in Scottish industrial history disappeared at that time. Half a billion pounds certainly cleared the slums, but the new industries didn't come – and the people left. It was *Last Exit from Brigton*.

Industrial Bridgeton has gone, but what has replaced it? A recent OECD (Organisation for Economic Co-operation and Development) report on Glasgow said it was developing a two-track economy: bands of regeneration and prosperity, alongside areas of continuing deprivation and exclusion; this certainly applies to the East End. Let's go walkabout. Take the train to Bridgeton Station and emerge into the light at Bridgeton Cross.

At the Cross itself is one of Glasgow's best cast-iron productions, the 50-feet-high Umbrella, complete with clock tower, originally built to shelter the unemployed in the depression of the 1870s. Unlike many public cast-iron works in Glasgow it was not produced at the Saracen Foundry in Possil, but by the Sun Foundry. One has to look hard, I admit, for an urban renaissance in the immediate vicinity of the Cross, with its ruins of the Olympia Cinema and the derelict Bridgeton Central Station, but there are many things of interest. In Landressy Street, next to the Public Library, stood till the mid-1980s the Bridgeton Working Men's Club. Clubs like this one, founded in 1865, though latterly becoming mainly drinking quarters, initially provided places of entertainment and instruction for the working man before 1914. The Bridgeton Club had a library of 2,000 volumes, mainly Victorian classics like Dickens, Scott and Burns, and took a selection of newspapers. But its main attraction would appear to have been the billiard hall, which raised half of the club's total income in 1902. In Bridgeton there was no more popular reading than the poems of Burns. The Bridgeton Burns Club, founded in 1870, became the largest in the world, with 1,400 members, and it sponsored competitions in local schools for the recitation and singing of the Bard's works. Burns himself visited Bridgeton, when it was still mainly a weaving suburb of Glasgow, staying at the Saracen's Head Inn in 1788.

People tend to think that the Glasgow tenements were always there, emerging as if from some prehistoric eruption. But till the 1870s and 1880s most of the city was still composed of lower terraced housing, detached houses or cottages. There is a wonderful painting by John Quinton Pringle, called *Muslin Street, Bridgeton*, executed in the 1880s. (This is in Edinburgh City Art Galleries, which fact I regard as an affront to this city.) At this time Bridgeton, annexed by Glasgow in 1846, was still mainly a textile producing area, though heavy industry was moving in. Its population had grown from about 4,000 in 1800 to 64,000 – and was still growing. A brass founder's with its ventilation slats is depicted in Pringle's painting of the street. Pringle shows us Bridgeton from the roof of his house, and we see one three-storey tenement, but mainly two-storey, white-harled and red-pantile-roofed housing, with the lums of the cotton mills in the background. Pringle, a highly skilled artisan (he was an optical repairer) was self-taught, but for me his superiority over his contemporary Glasgow Boys is undisputed. Muslin Street is just south of Bridgeton Cross. Take a Pringle print with you and compare the street today.

From the Cross, a stroll along London Road and then up Fielden Street takes you past some of the less imaginative 1970s council housing, and some of the best of more recent attempts at filling the vast waste sites in the area with new housing. Certainly it is a patchy picture, but Miles Better than the situation which appalled me on my arrival in Glasgow 30 years ago, well described by William Barr in *Glasgwegiana* (1973):

Thomas Sulman's 'Glasgow' *Illustrated London News* (1861)
Calton from the air

Industry is overwhelming the East End, but the university is still here,
and Monteith Row and Charlotte Street are still occupied by the cream
of Glasgow society, though not for much longer.

You are struck by the general scene of decay and neglect that pervades the area. Street after street of tall tenements stand empty, their shattered windows open and gaping to the sky. Broken glass lies in profusion on the streets ... and the unchecked running water floods into the street ... the engineering works, mills and factories have been closed down leaving Brigton with the appearance of a ghost town.

Turning back west along the Gallowgate you pass on one side St Mungo's Academy, recently renovated under the controversial Schools 2002 Private Public Partnership scheme, but balanced against that on the other side of the street is the once-smart Art Deco Bellgrove Hotel – now run-down and used as a Model Lodging House. Possibly not the best image opposite their school to encourage the young to a life of study. Next along is the former meat and cattle market, one of Glasgow's many nineteenth-century civic markets, whose façade has been lovingly retained though the market is no longer used. Aside from the stunning façade there are many things around here to look at. At the back end of Graham Square is the eighteenth-century inn (now housing) where the cattle dealers and drovers would reside during sales, while, outside, shawlie-women would queue for pails of blood with which to make black puddings and combat anaemia in their weans. While much of the huge site of the market remains sadly derelict and littered, Graham Square hosts a development of housing association properties of the highest social and architectural merit, which won a Saltire Award in 2001.

A walk up Bellgrove Street takes you to Duke Street. Turning west you soon pass below the Glasgow Necropolis. Though technically outwith Bridgeton, Glasgow's graveyard for its wealthy citizens is well worth a visit, especially now that it has been largely restored. Below it is found probably the only large-scale factory left in this area; the Tennent's Brewery, which, incidentally, must also be the oldest industrial undertaking in the city, dating from 1556. In the Necropolis are Gothic tombs and Byzantine-style mausoleums, some of which are bigger than the average single-end that most people in and around Bridgeton once inhabited. But that there were better-class tenements here is shown by the rosy sandstone survival on Hunter

Street, opposite the Tennent's Brewery, a fine building with elaborate bas-reliefs of the brewing trade (the tenement belonged to Tennents). It has to be admitted, though, that not many of the buildings in this area were of this standard, and few of the Victorian and Edwardian tenements remain.

But even Bridgeton had its social distinctions, its areas of better housing, and its areas of lesser reputation. Clifford Hanley, author of *Dancing in the Streets,* spent his first six years in Bridgeton, and was aware, or maybe had a maw who was aware, of fine social differentiations. South from the Gallowgate towards Bridgeton Cross was dangerous, north towards Dennistoun, safer, as he comments:

> South of Gallowgate meant Cubie Street and Soho Street, and I never went down Soho Street. It was always north that our wanderings took us, the north separated from Gallowgate by the railway.

Heading south again from Tennent's brewery by Barrack Street (so called because troops were stationed there from its construction in 1795 as a counter measure to local radicalism) takes you back to the Gallowgate and then past the Barrowland ballroom to the Barras, the world centre of reset goods, hucksters, conmen – and the odd bargain. In a bold move, a former clay pipe factory and subsequent warehouse next to the Barras has been coverted into flats for sale, in the middle price range, showing that regeneration is slowly reaching the obscurer corners of the city. Not maybe where you would want a granny flat or to breed babies, but if I was a single man and 30 years younger, I'd like living there. But a few steps further towards Glasgow Cross and you are reminded this is Glasgow, not Hampstead. The curiously named Shipka Pass (after a battle in a forgotten Balkan war) hosts a market whose proprietor Mr Barton clearly feels the Barras has sold out to Yuppiedom. Its signs display a weird mixture of erudition and self-revelling Glasgow grottiness. 'We Buy Rubbish and Sell Antiques', one sign proclaims, while others tell of the exploits of famous Scotsmen and Partick Thistle FC. Glasgow without such gallus cheek would not be the same. This is a prime development site, a spit from Glasgow Cross, and it is probably destined to disappear.

Cross the London Road from Shipka Pass and you are heading for St Andrews Square, which could be the surprise of your day if you don't know the city. A recent housing development in traditional style flanks the St Andrew's Church, one of the gems of Glasgow's ecclesiastic architecture, and now an arts centre and restaurant. The church, finished in 1757, was modelled on St Martin in the Fields in London to a design by Dreghorn and boasts magnificent rococo plasterwork inside. Just south on the corner of Greendyke Street is the Kirk of St Andrews by the Green, known as the Whistlin Kirk or the Piskie Kirk, finished seven years earlier. Apparently the first Episcopalian place of worship to be built in the city after 1689, the mason who built it was excommunicated by the Glasgow Presbytery; the fact that the Kirk had an organ gave it its name. Again imaginative thinking has restored it as Housing Association offices, and the graveyard has also been renovated. The existence of such prestigious kirks here reminds us that, unlike other industrial areas of Glasgow like Govan or Springburn, the East End developed beside, and then overwhelmed, an area inhabited by the upper echelons of the Dear Green Place. The University itself backed onto this area, till its scholars fled to the West End in the 1870s.

The Whistlin Kirk (as well as a pub of that name) faces Glasgow Green itself. Around the Green are social contradictions you would be hard put to find in any other city; Glasgow grot cheek by jowl with futuristic urban renewal. A stone's throw from the Green is Paddy's Market, where the poorest come and buy things most of us would be embarrassed at giving away. As far back as the 1870s, Tweed, in his *Guide to Glasgow and the Clyde*, observed 'a low wooden erection, sacred to the vending of old clothes, known as Paddy's Market. It is unsightly in its appearance, unpleasant in its associations, and it is to be hoped it will soon be removed'.

Tweed would be distressed to see that the market still flourishes. Throw the stone the other way from here towards Greendyke Street and we have the Homes for the Future, staggeringly effective models for urban living built for the Year of Architecture in 1999 – and snapped up despite the six-figure price tags, showing that many people want to live city centre. And whyever not? The view over the Green and the Clyde from these houses, to the Cathkin Braes in the far south, is

worth a mortgage itself. These new houses are amongst the best of contemporary Scottish architecture and fit well with the 1960s school next
to them, designed by Glasgow architect Coia, one of the few structures
worth preserving from that period. This is a fine building showing that
not all '60s architecture was bad; it is no longer a school, but offices.

Seeking refreshments in this region is an adventure. There is the
international fusion cuisine of the Café Source in St Andrews Kirk, or
under the disused railway bridge by Paddy's is a devil's kitchen *Snack
Bar*, serving ham ribs and cabbage to the market's shoppers and the
Salvation Army residents sheltering under the bridge. Where else can
such a choice of eateries – with just about everything in between – be
had in such a small area?

The Green is also a salutary reminder of many of the good things
about the old East End, which should not be forgotten. It was here
that the early trades unions held their demonstrations, from the striking Calton Weavers in 1787 to the UCS work-in in the 1970s, and this
was where the suffragettes and temperance fighters staged their ral-
lies. The Weavers' Strike of 1787 was the first major industrial
dispute in Glasgow's – or Scotland's – history. The cloth-masters cut
the price for the goods they put out to the weavers, and in and around
Glasgow they struck work. When the weavers organised a demonstration, the soldiers were called out and six weavers killed, though
only three of their names are known. These first martyrs of the
Scottish working class are buried in Bridgeton, in the graveyard in
Abercrombie Street. A commemorative plaque recalls the events,
though only one name is still legible, that of John Page. In this graveyard too lies the Rev James Smith, who was Abraham Lincoln's
minister, and later US consul in Scotland.

Despite the setback the weavers hereabouts were apparently not
cowed. Alexander Allan, one of the weaving capitalists, built himself
a mansion by the Clyde. Unlike his fellow weaving capitalist Harvie
(see the account of Harvie's Dyke in the Parkhead chapter), Allan did
not block off the riverside right of way. Instead he had it built over,
extending his gardens to the Clyde, but forcing walkers to pass
through the tunnel which he constructed over the path, known as
Allan's Pen. Outraged by this interference with their traditional access
to the river, the weavers refused to accept work from Allan, even when

he promised increased wages. Deeply troubled financially, Allan fled to Ireland, as Harvie was also to do. A Clyde flood swept most of the Pen away. Working people liked walking as a recreation, and resented any interference with their rights.

It is interesting that the first local guide to walking was written in Bridgeton, by Hugh MacDonald in 1854. His *Rambles round Glasgow* took MacDonald to many interesting places and for 50 years his was the main walking guide to the Glasgow area. Mac-Donald had been born in Bridgeton in 1817, one of 11 children, as was apprenticed as a calico-block-maker in the textile industry. He worked in Bridgeton in the Barrowfield works, where children were employed in the bleachfield for 18 pence a day. MacDonald was politically active and contributed to Chartist publications, later breaking into publishing as a contributor to the *Glasgow Citizen* newspaper, where many of his walks were published. He deserves to be better known, and should be, now that a gate on the redeveloped Green has been named after him.

MacDonald was especially attached to Glasgow Green and worried about the survival of its trees, since 'The Orient blasts come laden with death from the Bridgeton factories.' He was familiar with the local rights of way battles of Harvie's Dyke and Alan's Pen, and proud of the Green's political role:

> To the achievement of the great moral victory of 1832 (for in its fruits, which are not yet all reaped, it has indeed been great,) the magnificent meetings on Glasgow Green must have contributed in no little degree.

The Green's role in political protest continued afterwards. In 1838 a huge demonstration took place on Glasgow Green, in support of the People's Charter, which advocated universal male suffrage. Seventy trades unions with banners took part. The Glasgow Universal Suffrage Association was a moderate group, on the moral force wing of Chartism. It faded away after 1842, its remaining members tuning to campaigns for teetotalism and to the formation of Chartist Churches, of which one was established in Bridgeton. But Chartism revived in the hungry year of 1848, inspired by the Revolution in France, and in Bridgeton the barricades went up.

In February a crowd gathered on the Green and demanded a minimum wage of two shillings a day; the city magistrates offered soup tickets instead. Later the crowd tore down the iron railings of Monteith Row, and sacked shops for food and arms, advancing on the city centre. One eye witness recalled later:

> In the year of 1848 I witnessed a procession of a large body of ill-fed, ill-clad and half armed Chartists, men women and boys, enter Buchanan Street. The procession turned sharp down the street and when passing Gordon Street fired two shots in the air.

Another states:

> This outbreak soon assumed an alarming aspect. The mob had rapidly increased, and shops were entered and robbed by the hungry people. A gunsmith in Exchange Square was entered and guns and ammunition carried off.

Police, troops and special constables charged the rioters and drove them from the High Street and Saltmarket, arresting 150. The next day soldiers parading through Bridgeton were attacked, and a barricade was thrown up across the Gallowgate. This was assaulted by troops and broken down, and after a subsequent series of exchanges of fire six demonstrators were shot and an unspecified number killed. Two alleged ringleaders of the troubles, Smith and Crosson, were summarily tried and given 10 and 18 years' transportation by Sheriff Allison (J Campbell *Recollections of Radical Times,* 1880).

The Green was always a demotic place, the population originally having the right to dry their clothes and graze their animals on it, and later with the Glasgow Fair spilled onto the Green from the 1840s. *The Sports o Glasgow Green* tells of Jocky and Jenny spending a day at the fair:

> There were spinners, and clippers and darners
> Some rogues and some decent folk
> The chiels were a' merrily playing
> At prick the loop, dice and black jock.

Punch and Judy shows, exhibitions of dwarfs with a giant 'frae the Kingdom o Fife', and a menagerie are all part of the fun till they repair Lucky McNee's in Clyde Street. Then:

Forfauchten wi drinking and dancing
The twa they cam toddlin haim
Wi rugging and riving and drawing
They baith were wearied and lame.

Another song, *Bonnie Glasgow Green,* tells the most improper story of a lad, from Aberdeen I regret to say, who steals away the affections of a girl spreading her clothes on the Green. Despite the fact that she is engaged to a local mason, 'my Jamie that hews the stane/Tae mak oor toon look braw', the girl goes off with the Aberdonian. I have never found the local women as accommodating.

Generations of tanner ba' football enthusiasts honed their skills there. The Green was the first home of Rangers FC, and even today Bridgeton and Rangers are held, shall we say, to have a certain special relationship. It is fitting that Glasgow's People's Palace, a museum to

Muirhead Bone *Glasgow; Fifty Drawings* (1911)
Barrows Market, Plate 25
Actually called Paddy's Market. An affront to the respectable since the middle
of the nineteenth century, 'Paddy's' was originally held beside the Clyde. It still
operates, in an alleyway behind the Justiciary Buildings.
Glasgow City Council (Museums)

its rich working-class life, is located there, and that a major renewal programme is preparing the Green for this new century, supported by Heritage Lottery and Scottish National Heritage funding. Central to this is the restoration of the Doulton Fountain from the Empire Exhibition of 1888, repaired and relocated within the Palace. Described as 'an exuberant terracotta wedding cake' it celebrates an Empire at its apogee; that a bolt of lightning shattered Victoria at its summit in 1894 was possibly a reminder that nothing lasts for ever.

Glasgow's East End has traditionally put its best face to the Green, with the now-vanished Monteith Row being originally composed of grand town houses; these later were converted into slum warrens and are now all gone, apart from one building which houses a 'hotel', often, as in this case, a euphemism hereabouts for a lodging house. Yet a few hundred yards away is the Inn on the Green, one of Glasgow's most upmarket eateries and hotels. Another prestige address was Charlotte Street, where town mansions housed entrepreneurs such as David Dale, one of the founders of Glasgow's cotton industry. One house in this street, built in 1782, has thankfully been saved by conversion into housing association dwellings – winning another Saltire Award in 1990. Dale's dwelling, which would have been very similar, was demolished to make way for a car park. JG Lockhart, Walter Scott's son-in-law and biographer, died in Charlotte Street, while John Stuart Blackie, the eminent Greek scholar, was born there.

At the eastern end of the Green there is another example of this area's rich built legacy, one of the world's most amazing factories – Templeton's carpet factory, now, like so many of the industries of the past, closed. William Leiper's 1889 design, based on the Doge's Palace in Venice, and faced in polychrome brick, overcame the initial resistance of the Council to have a factory on the Green itself, and the city council duly purchased its carpets from Templeton's for decades. What is less well known is that a fault in design led to the collapse of the façade, killing 29 workers, and it had to be rebuilt. The factory has escaped demolition by being converted into offices and smaller workspaces, and appears destined to undergo yet another reinvention as luxury flats. None in the world would have a finer façade.

A short distance east of Templeton's on McPhail Street is the former Greenview School, a splendid building, originally the mansion of the cotton baron MacPhail, and dating from 1846. The philanthropist James Buchanan left £30,000 for its conversion into a school 'for the maintenance and instruction of destitute children'. The year after the Education Act of 1872, which made education compulsory, the delightful 'Young Scholar in Studious Pose' was carved in sandstone by William Brodie and placed atop the building. This, along with the adjacent Logan and Johnstone School of Domestic Economy, which a Beehive bas-relief tells us was 'Instituted in 1890', provided instruction for generations of Bridgeton bairns, but both have long been surplus to requirements. They are in the process of being converted into flatted dwellings, to bring new life to old buildings, and help arrest the area's depopulation.

A pleasant continuation to the Shawfield Bridge brings the Green to an end. Here at Flesher's Haugh can be found a headless statue of James Watt, whose epoch-making discoveries regarding the development of a separate condenser for the steam engine, came to him while walking hereabouts. It was his invention that allowed industry to move into towns from the water-powered countryside, and laid the basis for the industrialisation of Glasgow. Surely his headless torso is no fitting memorial? Or maybe, given de-industrialisation, it actually is.

As one heads northwards to Bridgeton Cross up Main Street, the adjoining Mill Street, Poplin Street and Muslin Street (and Dale Street) remind you that before heavy engineering this was cotton country, and hereabout lie the gaunt ruins of former mills, such as the huge Carstairs Street Cotton Mill, awaiting a new use, or more likely demolition. As spinning was mechanised, domestic spinning declined and the trade moved into factories, many of which were in the East End. Bridgeton was a centre of the cotton–spinners' strike in the 1830s, the details of which are given in the chapter on Anderston. At first mechanised spinning increased the number of handloom weavers, but that trade too was soon mechanised and weaving, like spinning, transferred largely to factory production.

The weaving period left its legacy of song. Many will have heard the words of the *Calton Weaver*, which was written here. The author tells us:

Ah'm a weaver a Calton weaver
Ah'm a rash and a rovin blade
I've got siller in ma pooches
I'll gae follae the rovin trade

But after an encounter with drink (Nancy Whisky), he repents:

Ah'l gae back tae the Calton weavin
Ah'l fairly mak the shuttles fly
For ah'l mak mair at the Calton weavin
Than ever I did in a rovin wye

But not so many know that Alex Rodger, another weaver-poet, wrote *The Muckin o Geordies Byre* in Bridgeton. So the areas musical traditions are not only those of Billy-Boy doggerel.

But it is impossible to ignore this in Bridgeton. When my fellow Aberdonian, Paton, came to Glasgow in the early twentieth century, he lived in Bridgeton for a while and commented on the sectarianism he found here, in his fascinating autobiography, *Proletarian Pilgrimage*. As a socialist he initially 'watched this faction fight with a pitying contempt for both sides' – until the Orangemen began to cause trouble at the ILP meetings at Bridgeton Cross. Unlike in Partick where this turned violent, Paton observed of the Orangemen that 'In Bridgeton, their opposition, although a nuisance, never went beyond noisy interruption'. After 1918 Orangeism in Bridgeton degenerated into lumpen-proletarian criminality and gang warfare, wonderfully depicted in Edwin Morgan's poem *King Billy*, on the death of a gang leader.

Go from the grave. The shrill flutes
Are silent, the march dispersed.
Deplore what is to be deplored,
And then find out the rest.

Before the war Paton tells us in *Proletarian Pilgrimage* the Bridgeton ILP were a small group of about 40 people; in 1922 James Maxton won Bridgeton for the ILP with about 60% of the vote. And it was a protest at housing conditions as much, if not more, than industrial exploitation, which swept Maxton to power. This issue gained especial importance with the winning of the vote in 1918 by a large sector of the female population, and was one on which Maxton fought hard. Maxton was not from Bridgeton, but he taught in Green Street School here and represented the area in Westmister from 1922 till his death in 1946. They used to say they weighed, not counted, his votes, and he was revered and loved by the local population.

Calton's song writing traditions have continued with the works of the late Matt McGinn. He was an activist in the Communist party, which he later left, and wrote songs in support of many working-class struggles such as the UCS work-in. One of the songs he wrote actually takes its inspiration from a weavers' refrain, though *If it Wisnae for the Weavers* is from Forfarshire, not Calton. In the affluent '60s McGinn reminded his fellow workers of their past struggles:

Too ra loo ra loo ra loo
I'll tell ye something awfu' true
Ye wouldnae hae yer telly the noo
It it wisnae for the Unions.

Before going to Ruskin College and becoming a teacher McGinn worked in various places on Clydeside, including the GKN factory in Hillington. This was reputed 'the noisiest factory in Britain' and McGinn had only been there two days when he initiated a strike. McGinn would surely not have been without an observation in song about the disappearance of his old slum birthplace, and its replacement by loft appartments.

Calton may be going upmarket, central Bridgeton seems to be more or less holding its own, but Dalmarnock, between Bridgeton and Parkhead, appears to be losing its battle at the moment. Dalmarnock is now mainly wasteland with the odd festering ghetto and isolated multi-storey block emerging from the dereliction. Around this area signs of regeneration are few, and we are definitely in the land of dookits and back-alley boxing clubs. Yet Dalmarnock was once booming, the site of many industries, including one only second in the East End to Beardmore's in Parkhead, the Dalmarnock Iron Works. These were established by William Arrol in the 1870s, at a huge site with its own railway sidings, between Dalmarnock Road and London Road. Here up to 5,000 men earned their bread. Arrol was Scotland's greatest engineer since Telford. The firm made cranes and steel fabrication machinery, but Arrol was mainly a structural engineer, and himself built many of the factories of Glasgow's heavy industry period. Arrol's main memorials are the Forth Railway Bridge, and then the replacement Tay Railway Bridge, as well as London's Tower Bridge.

These fine bridges all remain, but what remains in Dalmarnock? I was pleased to see that Stoddart's bedding factory does, employing a dozen people. I came here as a young married man in the 1970s to buy a bed, on my first trip to darkest Dalmarnock. (I used to come later to get my mountain boots repaired by a couple of old cobblers who were members of the Creag Dhu climbing club; they have now gone). Anyway I ordered the bed from the sales agent and asked for it to be delivered to my address. Being asked where that was, I though the best response would be to mention a location known throughout the western world. 'Near Partick,' I said. 'Is that in Glasgow?' was the salesperson's reply. Despite the limited geography of their then sales rep, the firm has survived.

Walk along Springfield road to London Road, to the edge of Bridgeton where Celtic Park comes into view, and then head westwards along London Road itself. Soon we are back at the Cross where we started a couple of hours ago, and we have only scratched the surface of this fascinating area. I have not even mentioned the Saracen Head Inn, built in 1754, where the old stagecoach used to depart for its 12-day journey to London (or the Sarry Heid as it is locally known – even Sorry Heid by hangover sufferers). Wordsworth – as well as Johnson and Boswell – visited here at the time when it was the rendezvous of the town's elite. A huge five-gallon punch bowl from the Sarry Heid, now in the People's Palace, commemorates the drinking bouts of those days. The East End may never become a major tourist destination but in a couple of miles radius from Bridgeton Cross there is more to see and think on than in many, indeed any, of the more salubrious areas of Glasgow.

Being located so close to the city's thriving centre, with its expanding commercial and cultural activities and increased demand for housing, Bridgeton, or at least the western part of it, is better placed than many other post-industrial areas to benefit from Glasgow's re-invention of itself as a city of the future rather than the past. But real problems remain. The good jobs in the post-industrial city are not ones for which Bridgeton's residents are qualified. And we cannot forget that Bridgeton lies within that Glasgow which is the cancer and heart-attack capital of Europe. But walking around its streets does not cause me despair, though it causes me occasional anger; when in places like Dalmarnock I ask myself, what did these people do to deserve being treated as they have been? I always return from Bridgeton uplifted. There is room for optimism if the motto of the Bridgeton Working Men's Club is followed:

LEARN FROM THE PAST
USE WELL THE FUTURE

Index

Some other books published by **LUATH** PRESS

Mountain Days & Bothy Nights

Dave Brown and Ian Mitchell
ISBN 0 946487 15 4 PBK £7.50

Acknowledged as a classic of mountain writing still in demand ten years after its first publication, this book takes you into the bothies, howffs and dosses on the Scottish hills. Fishgut Mac, Desperate Dan, Stumpy and the Big Yin stalk hill and public house, evading gamekeepers and Royalty with a camaraderie which was the trademark of Scots hillwalking in the early days.

The fun element comes through... how innocent the social polemic seems in our nastier world of today... the book for the rucksack this year.
Hamish Brown, SCOTTISH MOUNTAINEERING CLUB JOURNAL

The doings, sayings, incongruities and idiosyncrasies of the denizens of the bothy underworld... described in an easy philosophical style... an authentic word picture of this part of the climbing scene in latter-day Scotland, which, like any good picture, will increase in charm over the years.
Iain Smart, SCOTTISH MOUNTAINEERING CLUB JOURNAL

The ideal book for nostalgic hillwalkers of the '60s, even just the armchair and public house variety... humorous, entertaining, informative, written by two men with obvious expertise, knowledge and love of their subject.
SCOTS INDEPENDENT

Mountain Outlaw

Ian R Mitchell
ISBN 1 84282 027 3 £6.50

The amazing story of Ewan MacPhee, Scotland's last bandit.
In 1850 Ewan MacPhee of Glenquoich, these islands' last outlaw, died awaiting trial in jail in Fort William. This was a man who:
– had been forced to enlist at the time of the Napoleonic wars, and deserted
– lived as an outlaw and rustler in Lochaber for over twenty years
  – had several capital offences hanging over his head
  – was a hero to the local peasantry at the time of the Clearances
  – abducted a wife – who later became his firmest ally

MacPhee has fascinated Ian R Mitchell for many years. He has sifted the surviving information on the outlaw, examined many of the legends associated with him, and bridged the gaps with an imagination of great authenticity, to produce *Mountain Outlaw*, a historical-creative account of MacPhee's life.

The author has done a superb job in collating what little has been written about MacPhee... and has produced a mixture of fact and well-informed fiction to give us more than just a glimpse of the man's extraordinary life.
SCOTS MAGAZINE

. . . Packed with as much adventure, murder and mayhem as any work of fiction . . .
PRESS AND JOURNAL

Scotland's Mountains before the Mountaineers

Ian R Mitchell
ISBN 0 946487 39 1 PBK £9.99

Who were the first people to 'conquer' Scotland's mountains, and why did they do it?
Which clergyman climbed all the Cairngorm 4,000-ers nearly two centuries ago?
How many Munros did Bonnie Prince Charlie bag?

Which bandit and sheep rustler hid in the mountains while his wife saw off the sheriff officers with a shotgun?
According to Gaelic tradition, how did an outlier of the rugged Corbett *Beinn Aridh Charr* come to be called *Spidean Moirich*, 'Martha's Peak'?
Who was the murderous clansman who gave his name to *Beinn Fhionnlaidh*?

In this ground breaking book, Ian Mitchell tells the story of explorations and ascents in the Scottish Highlands in the days before mountaineering became a popular sport – when bandits, Jacobites, poachers and illicit distillers used the mountains as sanctuary. The book also gives a detailed account of the map makers, road builders, geologists, astronomers and naturalists, many of whom ascended hitherto untrodden summits while working in the Scottish Highlands.

Scotland's Mountains before the Mountaineers is divided into four Highland regions, with a map of each region showing key summits. While not designed primarily as a guide, it will be a useful handbook for walkers and climbers. Based on a wealth of new research, this book offers a fresh perspective that will fascinate climbers and mountaineers and everyone interested in the history of mountaineering, cartography, the evolution of landscape and the social history of the Scottish Highlands.

... at last a work which does justice to those who lived and worked, travelled and fought in the Highlands before (and after) Walter Scott ... an important new revision of a fascinating topic.
PROFESSOR BRUCE LENMAN, from his foreword to *Scotland's Mountains before the Mountaineers.*

On the Trail of Queen Victoria in the Highlands

Ian R Mitchell
ISBN 0 946487 79 0 PBK £7.99

How many Munros did Queen Victoria bag?
What 'essential services' did John Brown perform for Victoria?
(And why was Albert always tired?)
How many horses (to the nearest hundred) were needed to undertake a Royal Tour?
Q: What happens when you send a republican on the tracks of Queen Victoria in the Highlands?
A: You get a book somewhat more interesting than the usual run of the mill royalist biographies!

Ian R Mitchell took up the challenge of attempting to write with critical empathy on the peregrinations of Vikki Regina in the Highlands, and about her residence at Balmoral, through which a neo-feudal fairyland was created on Upper Deeside. The expeditions, social rituals and iconography of that world are explored and exploded from within, in what Mitchell terms a Bolshevisation of Balmorality. He follows in Victoria's footsteps through-out the Cairngorms and beyond, to the further reaches of the Highlands. On this journey, a grudging respect and even affection for Vikki ('the best of the bunch') emerges.

The book is designed to enable the armchair/motorised reader, or walker, to follow in the steps of the most widely-travelled royal personage in the Highlands since Bonnie Prince Charlie had wandered there a century earlier.

Includes:
– Index map and 12 detailed maps.
– 21 walks in Victoria's footsteps.
– Rarely seen Washington Wilson photographs.
– Colour and black and white reproductions of contemporary paintings.

Luath Press Limited
committed to publishing well written books worth reading

LUATH PRESS takes its name from Robert Burns, whose little collie Luath (Gael., swift or nimble) tripped up Jean Armour at a wedding and gave him the chance to speak to the woman who was to be his wife and the abiding love of his life. Burns called one of The Twa Dogs Luath after Cuchullin's hunting dog in Ossian's Fingal. Luath Press was established in 1981 in the heart of Burns country, and is now based a few steps up the road from Burns' first lodgings on Edinburgh's Royal Mile.
Luath offers you distinctive writing with a hint of unexpected pleasures.

Most bookshops in the UK, the US, Canada, Australia, New Zealand and parts of Europe either carry our books in stock or can order them for you. To order direct from us, please send a £sterling cheque, postal order, international money order or your credit card details (number, address of cardholder and expiry date) to us at the address below. Please add post and packing as follows: UK – £1.00 per delivery address; overseas surface mail – £2.50 per delivery address; overseas airmail – £3.50 for the first book to each delivery address, plus £1.00 for each additional book by airmail to the same address. If your order is a gift, we will happily enclose your card or message at no extra charge.

ILLUSTRATION: IAN KELLAS

Luath Press Limited
543/2 Castlehill
The Royal Mile
Edinburgh EH1 2ND
Scotland
Telephone: 0131 225 4326 (24 hours)
Fax: 0131 225 4324
email: gavin.macdougall@luath.co.uk
Website: www.luath.co.uk